Lanai and Molokai Travel and Adventure Guide

The Ultimate Shortcut to Thrills, Beauty, and Culture, and Authentic Experiences

Ocean Breeze Adventures

Copyright © 2025 by Diana Freel
All rights reserved.

Published by **Freel Publishing LLC**, doing business as **Ocean Breeze Adventures**
www.OceanBreezeAdventures.com

No part of this publication may be reproduced, distributed, or transmitted in any form or by any means, including photocopying, recording, or other electronic or mechanical methods, without prior written permission from the publisher, except for brief quotations used in reviews or critical articles.

ISBN (eBook): 978-1-964448-24-4
ISBN (Paperback): 978-1-964448-22-0
ISBN (Hardcover): 978-1-964448-23-7

Cover design, layout, and interior formatting by Freel Publishing LLC.

This book is a work of nonfiction. Every effort has been made to ensure accuracy at the time of publication; however, details such as business hours, pricing, and accessibility may change without notice. Readers are encouraged to verify information directly with local sources before traveling.

Printed or distributed worldwide through independent publishing platforms.

Dedication

To my wife, Skip—

You always had my back and made every day of our twenty years together an adventure.

To my son, Davey—

I miss you every day and know you are with me always.

Contents

About Ocean Breeze Adventures	1
1. Where the Map Ends, and the Journey Begins	2
2. Accessibility on Lānaʻi and Molokaʻi	8
3. Discovering Lanai and Molokai	12
4. Cultural Immersion	20
5. Planning Your Itinerary	34
6. Outdoor Adventures	48
7. Navigating the Islands	57
8. Culinary Delights	69
9. Accommodation Insights	78
10. Local Culture and Traditions	86
11. Hidden Gems and Offbeat Experiences	98
12. Safety and Practical Advice	112
13. Sustainability and Responsible Travel	125
14. Visual Storytelling and Photography	140
15. Conclusion-The Story that Stays With You	152
Continue Your Island Adventure	158
Ocean Breeze Adventures Travel Agency	160

About Ocean Breeze Adventures

Diana Freel—writer, adventurer, and founder of **Freel Publishing LLC** and **Ocean Breeze Adventures**—has dedicated her life to two powerful passions: travel and storytelling.

Winner of the *International Book Impact Award* for her *Maui Travel & Adventure Guide,* Diana's love for exploration began the moment she could travel freely, documenting her journeys as she explored the world.

Her path, however, hasn't been without challenges. In the late 1990s, Diana faced immense personal hardship and loss that reshaped her outlook on life. Through courage, resilience, and an unshakable spirit, she rebuilt her life and discovered a new calling: helping others heal and reconnect through the power of travel.

For Diana, travel became a source of renewal—a way to breathe, connect, and rediscover freedom. Each destination inspired her to see the world not just as a map of places, but as a canvas of stories waiting to be lived.

Today, through **Ocean Breeze Adventures**, Diana combines her passion for storytelling with her expertise in trip design, empowering travelers to explore with confidence and joy. Whether you're discovering the hidden gems of Hawaii, the wild beauty of Alaska, or tropical escapes beyond, her guides are created to make every journey meaningful, accessible, and transformative.

To learn more about Diana and explore more destinations, visit **www.OceanBreezeAdventures.com**

Chapter One

Where the Map Ends, and the Journey Begins

There are places in the world that whisper rather than shout. Places where the beauty is subtle, the pace is slow, and the stories aren't printed on brochures—they're passed quietly from hand to hand, voice to voice. Lanai and Molokai are two such places.

When you arrive, it's not with fanfare. There are no neon-lit welcome centers or choreographed greetings. You step off a ferry or land on a quiet tarmac, and the first thing you hear is wind through ironwood trees or the hush of ocean pulling back from shore. It's as if the land itself is pausing to look at you before deciding what to share.

The beaches here don't come with cabanas and cocktail service. They come with footprints that fade quickly and driftwood shaped by decades of tide. The trails don't lead to high-rise lookouts but to vistas you'll likely have to yourself. And the culture? It's not a performance. It's lived—daily, quietly, powerfully.

Lanai and Molokai are not just less visited—they are less altered. And in a world where tourism often smooths away the edges, that makes them rare. This book is a guide for those who are ready to explore that rarity with care, curiosity, and respect.

What This Book Offers

This is not a typical travel guide. You won't find top-ten lists or "must-do" countdowns here. Instead, you'll find a layered, thoughtful invitation into the heart of two islands that have held fast to their roots.

Across these pages, I'll walk you through the rich culture, adventure opportunities, culinary traditions, and practical travel tips specific to Lanai and Molokai. You'll learn where to hike for views that feel like secrets, how to snorkel responsibly in pristine waters, what to know before entering sacred spaces, and how to participate meaningfully in cultural events—whether through a hula demonstration or helping clear a taro patch.

You'll also find insights into sustainable travel practices, local businesses worth supporting, and the etiquette that transforms you from a visitor into a welcomed guest.

This is a guide designed for conscious travelers—those who seek more than just beautiful photos. It's for people who want experiences that last because they're grounded in real connection.

Why I Wrote This Book

My own journey with these islands began not with a plan, but with a feeling. A pull.

I was already a traveler and a storyteller, chasing down edges of the map and trying to make sense of the world through the lens of place. But Lanai and Molokai weren't originally on my itinerary. They found their way into my life through conversations—locals describing family land, friends reminiscing about childhood summers, artists talking about silence as muse.

When I finally visited, I understood. These islands don't just invite you in—they invite you inward. They ask for your presence. Your patience. Your openness.

On Lanai, I wandered pine-covered trails that smelled like rain and sap, watched sunset from a red-rock outcropping that looked more like Mars than Hawaii, and spoke with people who could describe a tree's history the way others describe a city skyline. On Molokai, I helped clear brush from a loʻi kalo under the watchful gaze of an elder who offered guidance in three words or less. I danced at a backyard party where the only music was a guitar passed between friends. And I felt, over and over again, that I was being trusted with something rare.

That trust is what shaped this book. It's my way of honoring what I was given and helping others receive it, too—without trampling it.

A Brief Look Back

To understand Lanai and Molokai, it helps to know where they've come from.

Lanai was once the world's largest pineapple plantation, shaped by the vision of James Dole and the labor of thousands. In 1922, Dole purchased the entire island, transforming its economy and landscape. Decades later, tech billionaire Larry Ellison acquired 98% of the island and began investing in sustainable infrastructure and luxury tourism—with mixed reactions from the local community. Today, Lanai stands at a unique intersection of development and preservation, where high-end wellness retreats sit within reach of wild, untouched terrain.

Molokai, by contrast, has resisted large-scale tourism. Known as "The Friendly Isle," it's a place where traditional Hawaiian values guide daily life. Community events are common, and the economy is deeply tied to agriculture, fishing, and family-owned businesses. Molokai also bears the weight of a difficult history—most notably the leprosy settlement at Kalaupapa, where thousands were exiled during the 19th and 20th centuries. That legacy has left a deep commitment to justice, compassion, and cultural continuity.

What unites both islands is their commitment to staying rooted. While much of Hawaii has evolved to accommodate visitors, Lanai and Molokai still ask visitors to adapt to them, not the other way around.

This Book is For You

If you're looking for all-inclusive resorts, packed luaus, and "Instagrammable" hot spots, this might not be the book for you.

But if you're someone who seeks quiet beauty, honest connection, and cultural respect, then you're in the right place.

This guide is written for adults who travel not just to see—but to understand. For those who believe that adventure is better when it's earned. For people who'd rather talk with a fisherman at the pier than check into a luxury suite (or at least do both with equal interest).

Whether you're traveling solo, as a couple, or with close friends, this book will help you move through these islands in a way that leaves space—for discovery, reflection, and the stories you can't always plan for.

What Makes This Guide Different

Many travel guides focus on logistics—flights, hours, and prices. And while we cover that too, this book goes deeper.

You'll find:

- Locally grounded insights gathered from real conversations and on-the-ground experiences.
- Sustainable travel principles designed to protect the islands and honor

community knowledge.

- Cultural etiquette guidance to help you show up with humility and leave with more than souvenirs.

- Flexible itineraries that prioritize quality over quantity.

This isn't a catalog of attractions. It's a map of mindset.

What You'll Find Inside

The chapters ahead will take you on a full-circle journey:

- **Chapter 1–2** introduce Lanai and Molokai through history, landscape, and culture.

- **Chapters 3–5** explore outdoor adventures, food experiences, and local art.

- **Chapters 6–7** guide you through accommodations, traditions, and ways to engage with community.

- **Chapters 8–10** offer practical insights on photography, planning itineraries, and discovering hidden gems.

- **Chapters 11–12** cover safety, wellness, and responsible travel, ensuring you not only enjoy your trip—but enrich it.

Each section is designed to give you tools, stories, and frameworks to travel more meaningfully.

A Gentle Challenge and a Warm Welcome

As you move through this book, I hope you'll do more than take notes. I hope you'll pause, reflect, and begin to think about how you want to move through the world—not just on these islands, but everywhere.

Ask yourself:

- What does it mean to be a respectful guest?
- What does adventure look like when you slow down?
- How might you carry what you learn here into other parts of your life?

This book is your invitation to travel differently. To notice more. To care more. To be changed—not just entertained.

Thank You for Being Here

I'm deeply grateful you've chosen this guide as a companion. Whether this is your first time visiting Hawaii or your tenth, Lanai and Molokai will show you something you haven't seen before—if you're willing to look with soft eyes and an open heart.

Thank you for traveling with intention. For listening before speaking. For stepping off the well-worn path and trusting that what you find there will be worth it.

Now, let's begin.

You're about to discover not just two islands—but a way of seeing the world that might just stay with you long after the journey ends.

Chapter Two

Accessibility on Lāna'i and Moloka'i

Lāna'i and Moloka'i are less developed than their bigger neighbors, but people with mobility issues or other special needs can still enjoy these islands if they plan ahead. Because the infrastructure here is smaller and based on the community, it's often necessary to plan ahead and know the area well to get around.

Ferries are a way to get around Lāna'i: Getting to the Expeditions ferry between Lāhainā (Maui) and Lāna'i is not very easy. The weather can make it harder to get on and off the board at times. Call ahead to ask for help and make sure you can get around.

Lāna'i has a small shuttle system that connects the ferry harbor, Lāna'i City, and the resorts. Some shuttles have lifts, but you should talk to your resort or shuttle provider ahead of time to make sure. Private drivers and taxis may be more flexible, but you should check to see if the car is available.

The most common type of rental car is a 4WD, but most of them don't work with hand controls. People who need cars that are easy to get into should call Lānaʻi Car Rental ahead of time.

Things to do

Lānaʻi City: The main town is small and mostly flat, but some sidewalks are bumpy. Some stores and restaurants are easier to get to than others.

Hulopoʻe Beach is the most accessible beach on the island. There is a flat surface, paved parking, and bathrooms. The Four Seasons Resort might have beach wheelchairs you can borrow. Find out by calling ahead.

Other Places: Attractions that are far away, like Keahiakawelo (Garden of the Gods) or Shipwreck Beach, are not wheelchair-friendly and require a 4WD vehicle and rough ground.

Staying at Four Seasons Resorts (Mānele Bay & Sensei): Have rooms that meet ADA standards, common areas that are easy to get to, and staff who know how to help. These are the best options for people who are traveling and need help getting around.

The Lānaʻi Hotel in Lānaʻi City is charming because of its history, but it's hard to get to. Before you book, make sure there are rooms available.

Molokaʻi

Getting around on Molokaʻi: The Molokaʻi Airport (MKK) has normal features for people with disabilities. Small planes fly to and from Honolulu or Maui, but there is help getting on board.

There aren't many shuttles or taxis on the island. Some drivers can fit foldable wheelchairs, but it's hard to find accessible vans. It is strongly suggested that you make a reservation ahead of time.

Renting a car: Not all rentals are available; most are small SUVs or trucks. People who have trouble getting around may need to ask friends or family for help or find other ways to get around.

Things to do: The main town of Kaunakakai is flat and has a few shops and restaurants that are easy to get to. However, the sidewalks may be narrow or uneven.

There is parking at Papohaku Beach, which is three miles long, but there aren't many paved paths. The sandy ground can make it hard to get to some places. There aren't many places that have beach wheelchairs.

Cultural Sites: Kalaupapa National Historical Park is not very easy to get to. People can't ride the mule, but they can fly in on a small plane. People in wheelchairs can explore the settlement with the help of a ranger once they get inside.

Hālawa Valley: You can only get there by taking a guided cultural hike, which isn't good for people who have trouble moving around.

Staying Vacation Rentals: There aren't as many options as there are on other islands. Before you book a private rental, make sure to read the fine print carefully, as many of them are not fully accessible.

Some of the rooms at Hotel Molokaʻi are accessible to people with disabilities, and the pool area has ramps, but not all of the property is accessible.

Helpful Tips for Traveling with Accessibility

Think Ahead: Because both islands don't have a lot of resources, make sure to check your accessibility needs well before you go.

Bring Important Gear: If you need things like beach wheelchairs or walkers to help you get around, you might want to bring your own or rent them from Maui before you go.

If you want amenities that meet the Americans with Disabilities Act (ADA), the best places to stay are big resorts like the Four Seasons (Lānaʻi) or Hotel Molokaʻi.

It's important to be able to change your mind: These islands value their natural beauty and rugged terrain, which is great for travelers who want to get away from it all, but some places may still be hard to reach. You can make your trip worth it by choosing the right things to do.

Chapter Three

Discovering Lanai and Molokai

There's something quietly magical about stepping onto an island where time doesn't rush. That's the feeling you get the moment you arrive on Lanai—a place where the buzz of tourism fades, and nature speaks in whispers. Unlike the more visited Hawaiian islands, Lanai remains largely untouched, its tranquility protected by remoteness and intention. With no traffic lights, no sprawling resorts crowding the beaches, and a population under 4,000, Lanai invites you into its stillness.

Getting here is part of the charm. With no direct flights from the mainland and limited ferry access, Lanai feels like a secret. This exclusivity creates a sense of intimacy—travelers come here not by accident, but by choice. And that choice rewards you with an experience that feels rare in today's fast-paced world.

If you're craving solitude, Hulopoe Bay is your introduction to serenity. Just a short ride from the ferry landing, this crescent-shaped beach is known for its crystal-clear waters and tide pools teeming with marine life. It's a protected marine preserve, which means the natural beauty is not only visible—it's thriving. You can snorkel alongside vibrant fish or simply sink into the soft sand with the sound of the ocean as your only companion. Even during busier seasons, it rarely feels crowded. This is where luxury and nature meet in the quietest way possible.

Then there's Lanai City, perched in the island's cool interior. It's not a "city" in the traditional sense—no skyscrapers, no rush hour, no neon signs. Instead, you'll find plantation-era architecture, shaded sidewalks, and a handful of locally owned cafes and galleries. Built in the 1920s by the Dole Pineapple Company, Lanai City was once the heart of what was known as the world's largest pineapple plantation. Today, it feels like a step back in time. Strolling through Dole Park, you'll find a community that values simplicity, where everyone seems to know each other and smiles come easily. There's an unspoken invitation to slow down and stay awhile.

Lanai's past is deeply rooted in agriculture, and James Dole played a central role in shaping its modern identity. In 1922, he purchased the entire island and turned it into a massive pineapple plantation. For decades, Lanai's economy—and landscape—revolved around pineapple production. That chapter eventually closed, but its legacy remains, not just in the land but in the character of the community.

In recent years, the island has seen a new chapter unfold under the stewardship of tech billionaire Larry Ellison, who purchased the majority of Lanai in 2012. His vision has leaned toward sustainable luxury and wellness-driven tourism. While this has brought investment and world-class accommodations, the core of Lanai's identity—quiet beauty, community warmth, and deep respect for the land—remains intact.

As you begin to explore the island, you'll notice how the natural landmarks feel both cinematic and sacred. One of the most unforgettable is Keahiakawelo, also known as the Garden of the Gods. Located on the northwest side of the island, this rocky expanse feels more like a Martian landscape than a tropical one. Massive boulders, twisted formations, and an orange hue that glows at sunset give the place an almost mystical energy. Hawaiian legends say this land was created by a contest between priests from Lanai and Molokai, each trying to keep a fire burning longer to prove spiritual power.

Just beyond lies Shipwreck Beach, a windswept stretch of sand on the northeastern shore. True to its name, the rusted shell of a World War II-era tanker still rests offshore, giving the coastline an eerie, storybook quality. The beach is more for wandering than swimming—strong currents make the water dangerous—but its isolation and historical aura make it unforgettable.

Lanai doesn't ask for your attention—it simply waits for you to notice it. From private guided tours to secluded hikes along the Munro Trail, everything here invites introspection. The Munro Trail, in particular, offers panoramic views stretching from Lanai to Molokai and even Maui on a clear day. The trail winds through pine forests and ridge lines, making it one of the island's most rewarding hikes—especially if you're looking for moments of quiet reflection.

What sets Lanai apart isn't just what's here, but what isn't. No crowds. No rush. No pressure to "do it all." Instead, you're offered the rare opportunity to experience an island that feels preserved—untouched, yet open-hearted. Whether you spend your days hiking alone, snorkeling in silence, or sipping coffee in Lanai City, the experience is deeply personal.

This is solitude by design—not isolation, but invitation. And for many travelers, that's exactly the escape they didn't know they needed.

Molokai—The Heartbeat of Hawaiian Culture

If Lanai whispers to the quiet in your soul, Molokai speaks to the roots beneath your feet. This is where the essence of Hawaii's past pulses through daily life, not in a curated exhibit, but in the hands of farmers, the songs of elders, and the rhythm of communal gatherings. Often overlooked by mainstream tourism, Molokai isn't for those seeking spa menus or luxury lounges—it's for those who want to feel the *mana*, the spiritual energy, that lives in the land and its people.

Here, tradition isn't packaged—it's practiced. On any given morning, you might see kupuna (respected elders) teaching children to dance hula, not for an audience, but for the ancestors. You may hear the steady beat of a pahu drum echoing from a school gymnasium or smell freshly cooked laulau being prepared for a family gathering. This is a place where you're not just welcome—you're invited to *listen*.

Daily life on Molokai is steeped in Hawaiian custom, not as a performance, but as a way of being. Farmers tend the land with ancestral methods, and fishers head out in outrigger canoes, guided by generations of knowledge passed down in quiet instruction. Even simple acts—gathering taro, mending fishing nets, chanting before sunrise—are treated with reverence. For travelers seeking authenticity, Molokai doesn't offer a show. It offers truth.

Community is not a concept here—it's a lived reality. Festivals on Molokai feel more like family reunions. Locals gather not just to celebrate but to connect, often with music, food, and heartfelt storytelling. If you find yourself at one of these gatherings, you'll likely be offered a plate of home-cooked food, a seat at the table, and a smile that asks for nothing in return. There's a quiet humility here that reshapes what hospitality means.

In the hills above the island's north shore lies a chapter of profound human history—Kalaupapa National Historical Park. Once a place of great suffering, it's now a sanctuary of remembrance and resilience. This isolated peninsula was home to individuals afflicted with Hansen's disease (leprosy), sent here by law during the 19th and 20th centuries. The legacy of Father Damien, a Belgian priest who gave his life in service to this community, is woven into the island's collective memory. His compassion earned him sainthood, but on Molokai, he is simply remembered as a man who stayed when others turned away.

Beyond the documented history, Molokai is rich with Hawaiian legend, including stories of the Menehune—a mythical race of small people believed to have built fishponds and temples overnight. Whether you take these tales as folklore or truth, they shape the landscape with meaning. Walking along a stone trail or sitting beside an ancient heiau (temple), you may feel something you can't quite name—and that's part of the island's gift.

Molokai also takes sustainability seriously, not as a tourism trend, but as a necessity. Locals understand that preservation is survival. You'll find eco-friendly tours led by community members, where protecting the land is more important than profit. Many guides are cultural practitioners themselves, offering insight not only into the terrain but also into the worldview that sustains it.

Conservation efforts stretch across the island, from reef restoration projects to native wildlife protection. You might stumble upon volunteers planting native flora on a hillside or join in a beach cleanup alongside schoolchildren and kupuna alike. These aren't photo ops—they're acts of commitment to future generations.

Molokai doesn't seek to impress you—it asks you to *participate*. Whether that means dancing at a local music event, shopping at a farmers market, or simply learning how to say "mahalo" with sincerity, your role here is not just that of a visitor. It's that of a guest entering someone's home—with respect, curiosity, and the willingness to leave changed.

On Molokai, you won't find five-star resorts or corporate luaus. But you will find five-star sunsets, stories carved into the cliffs, and a kind of quiet that helps you hear your own thoughts again. This island is not a destination—it's an invitation. One is to slow down, step into another way of life, and realize that the richest parts of a journey often have nothing to do with checklists or itineraries.

The Unique Allure of Undiscovered Hawaii

The stunning hotels of Waikiki and the coastal roads of Maui likely come to mind when you picture Hawaii. Although those images hold iconic status for good reasons, they capture only one aspect of the narrative. The quieter, richer, more intimate side of Hawaii exists in locations like Lanai and Molokai.

These islands don't compete with the spotlight. Their position just beyond the spotlight, combined with their contentment in subtlety, makes them unforgettable.

Tourists on Oahu and Maui frequently find themselves joining large tour groups and visiting packed beaches while following pre-established excursions. That sort of travel experience is perfectly fine. This location offers an authentic and unhurried experience through its expansive natural landscapes and itineraries formed from local interactions rather than tour books.

This version of Hawaii remains pristine and untouched. Beaches stand untouched by human activity, and coral reefs flourish with vibrant life in quiet abundance, whereas dense forests transport visitors to bygone eras.

When hiking trails on Lanai, you may continue for hours without encountering anyone else. A vast beach on Molokai offers a solitary experience with only wind and waves as your companions. In this place, you experience pure nature without any scripted scenes or background music, as your sole companions are you and the land.

The terrain itself tells stories. Rugged cliffs follow forest-covered hills as dry red earth unexpectedly transforms into oases. Hidden waterfalls and secluded bays often reveal themselves as if they were secrets only the wind and trees could know. Here, adventure doesn't feel engineered—it feels earned. Every discovery carries an awe-inspiring feeling because you find something that seemed to have been waiting specifically for you.

The excitement of venturing into uncharted territory becomes real when you choose an unseen route and find experiences that transcend brochure descriptions. The path could possibly lead to a historic trail decorated with ancient rock art or to a viewing spot that presents the islands with an unexpected illumination. There's no checklist for moments like that. And maybe that's the point.

The islands provide attractions beyond their stunning natural landscapes. Personal development becomes possible through the experiences these islands provide. When you're not distracted by crowds or consumed by your phone signal, you're left with space: these islands create opportunities for you to think deeply while taking deep breaths and reconnecting both with yourself and your surrounding environment. The islands of Lanai and Molokai inspire you to journey within yourself as much as you explore their landscapes.

The experience of discussing with a farmer about their fruit crop or sitting in quiet contemplation on a Pacific cliff connects you with ancient natural rhythms that surpass the fast pace of modern life. Travel goes beyond seeing new places because it allows these places to view you in return. You become aware of how you transform when you stop rushing through life.

These island communities maintain a close connection with the land while simultaneously fostering even tighter relationships among themselves. Their pace is different. The core values of their community focus on sustainability alongside stewardship and communal living. Entering that space with respect transforms you from an observer into an active participant. Together you enjoy meals and moments and occasionally exchange unspoken connections.

Modern travel experiences have become primarily entertainment-focused. Lanai and Molokai ask you to engage. They ask you to notice the quiet details: As you ascend a trail, you notice how the wind direction changes, and you hear the sound of a conch shell at sunset while feeling warm sand that remains untouched by footsteps. These aren't tourist attractions. They're invitations to presence.

These islands present a unique travel experience if you welcome the challenge. Slower. Deeper. With more curiosity and less expectation. Such travel experiences create personal stories that remain long after souvenirs have been forgotten.

Understanding the Aloha Spirit

The word "aloha" appears frequently throughout Hawaii. At the airport you encounter it as a greeting, while handwritten notes use it as a closing expression, and locals include it naturally in their conversations. Aloha serves as a greeting, yet its meaning extends far beyond simple salutations. This philosophy becomes a lifestyle that fundamentally invites you to connect with people, places, and meaningful purposes.

The word "aloha" functions as both a greeting and a farewell on the surface level. The essence of aloha reveals deep-rooted hospitality and mutual respect along with compassion. The Aloha Spirit represents unconditional giving and open-hearted living with welcoming acceptance. Travelers in Hawaii receive a lasting and meaningful gift when they experience aloha, and it becomes a powerful, lasting possession they take with them when departing.

The Aloha Spirit emerges through authentic connections between people. You receive a mango directly from a farmer who grows them on his own tree. The shopkeeper takes a break to narrate the history of a handcrafted local product. A young beach visitor extends a shell to you with complete silence. Visitors get to see authentic moments that reveal a culture centered around generosity and shared human experiences.

Involvement in community activities and traditional ceremonies provides another opportunity to observe this cultural base. Joining a hula performance or sharing a family-style luau meal and listening to a local chant at sunrise all bring intentional experiences.

Travelers who embody aloha leave lighter footprints—not just environmentally, but emotionally. They don't just pass through Hawaii. They become part of it, even if just for a while.

Before you step onto the trail or into the sea, take a moment to breathe deeply. Before you speak, think about kindness. Before you move forward, ask yourself if you're doing so with humility and care. That's the Aloha Spirit. It's not something you'll always find in guidebooks, but if you let it, it will shape your entire journey.

And perhaps, when your trip is over, you'll carry it with you—not just as a memory, but as a way of seeing the world a little differently.

Chapter Four

Cultural Immersion

There's a rhythm to Hawaii that you don't just hear—you feel it. On Molokai and Lanai, cultural traditions aren't performances for tourists; they're living, breathing parts of daily life. You'll notice it in the way locals greet each other with deep sincerity, in the gatherings that begin with quiet reverence, and in the sense of community that pulses through every celebration.

Traditional Hawaiian Ceremonies and Festivals

To truly connect with these islands, you don't just observe the culture—you participate in it.

The Sacred Ritual of Ho'oponopono

One of the most powerful cultural practices you'll encounter is Ho'oponopono, an ancient Hawaiian method of reconciliation and forgiveness. The word itself means "to make things right," and that's exactly what the ritual aims to do—restore balance between individuals, families, and even within oneself. Traditionally led by a respected elder or healer, the ceremony is a guided process where participants speak their truths, ask for forgiveness, and seek emotional harmony.

While not commonly open to visitors in its intimate, familial form, some cultural centers on Molokai offer introductory workshops or demonstrations that explain the philosophy behind Hoʻoponopono. You don't have to attend a full ceremony to learn from it—just understanding its core message of accountability, forgiveness, and healing can shift how you move through your travels and relationships.

A Glimpse into a Traditional Hawaiian Wedding

Imagine a serene beach, gently rustling palm fronds, and the melodic sound of a conch shell signaling the start of a Hawaiian wedding. These ceremonies are often more spiritual than religious, deeply rooted in the land and the culture. A traditional Hawaiian wedding might include the tying of a maile lei to symbolize unity, blessings spoken in ʻŌlelo Hawaiʻi, and offerings to the elements—water, wind, fire, and earth.

Even if you're not planning a wedding yourself, attending or witnessing one can be an unforgettable experience. On Molokai, where community ties run deep, guests may be invited to observe these heartfelt ceremonies during local events or festivals. It's a beautiful reminder of how Hawaiian culture sees relationships not just as a union between two people, but as a joining of families, spirits, and legacies.

Festivals that Celebrate the Soul of the Islands

If you're hoping to experience authentic Hawaiian culture in full bloom, plan your trip around one of the islands' annual festivals. The Molokai Ka Hula Piko Festival is especially powerful. Held in Kaunakakai, this celebration honors the birthplace of hula and includes cultural workshops, food vendors, and performances by hula practitioners from across the state. It's not a tourist spectacle—it's a gathering of people who carry the tradition in their hearts.

Another standout is the annual Aloha Festivals, which are celebrated across Hawaii, including select events on Lanai. These festivals highlight Hawaiian music, dance, and storytelling. You'll find parades, concerts, and street parties that welcome visitors not just as spectators, but as participants. What sets these events apart is their community-first focus—locals celebrate for themselves, and travelers are simply invited along for the ride.

How to Participate Respectfully

You don't need to know every protocol to be respectful—you just need to show up with curiosity and humility. If you attend a luau, for example, understand that not all luaus are created equal. Look for community-led events rather than commercial productions. These tend to be more authentic, with home-cooked meals, traditional chants, and even opportunities to learn a few hula steps.

For more sacred observances like makahiki, the Hawaiian New Year festival, it's important to follow local cues. Some events are closed to outsiders, while others welcome respectful observers. If invited to attend, dress modestly, ask before taking photos, and consider offering a small gift or donation if it feels appropriate. These small gestures speak volumes.

Ceremonies Reflecting Core Hawaiian Values

When you step into a Hawaiian ceremony or festival, you're entering a space where the island's deepest values are brought to life. Family ('ohana), respect (aloha), responsibility (kuleana), and harmony with nature (malama 'āina) aren't abstract ideas here—they're threads woven through every ritual.

You'll notice how family and community take center stage. Ceremonies often involve multiple generations, with elders guiding the process and children participating alongside adults. Festivals are built around communal effort—everyone has a role, from food preparation to music.

Nature is always present, too. Whether it's the location of the event, the materials used in the ceremony, or the chants that honor the wind and the sea, there's a spiritual connection to the land that grounds everything.

A Personal Glimpse Into Molokai's Heartbeat

On a trip to Molokai, I stumbled upon the Ka Hula Piko Festival entirely by chance. I'd planned a quiet morning walk through Kaunakakai but followed the sound of live drums and laughter to a grassy field dotted with food tents and handmade crafts. What started as curiosity turned into one of the most moving cultural moments of my journey.

I stood at the edge of the crowd as a group of hula dancers took the stage—some barely old enough to walk, others well into their sixties, all moving in sync with ancient chants. There were no spotlights, no grand stage production—just a reverent silence broken only by the rhythm of the pahu drum and the storyteller's voice. You could feel the mana, the spiritual energy, rise from the earth and settle over the gathering like a blessing.

Later that afternoon, I spoke with one of the musicians, an older man named Kaipo, who shared that his family had been performing at the festival for three generations. "We don't do this for show," he said, tuning his ukulele. "We do it so our kids remember who they are."

That one sentence stuck with me long after I left. It wasn't just about entertainment—it was about preserving identity through celebration. And as an outsider, I wasn't just a spectator. I was welcomed, fed, taught, and reminded that culture isn't something you take photos of—it's something you honor.

Arts and Crafts — The Soul of Lanai and Molokai

Art in Lanai and Molokai isn't confined to galleries or gift shops. It's carved into wood, woven into lauhala, painted across concrete walls, and etched into skin.

These islands carry a quiet but vivid current of creativity that flows through everything—from ancestral crafts to contemporary expression. When you explore the art of these islands, you're not just admiring aesthetics—you're experiencing culture, history, and identity made visible.

You'll notice quickly that art here often feels personal. Many artists in Lanai and Molokai don't separate their work from their way of life. Creativity is intertwined with family, community, and tradition. Whether it's a simple lei woven from native plants or a mural stretching across a local school building, the goal is the same: to honor the past while speaking to the present.

A Living Tradition of Craftsmanship

One of the most enduring art forms you'll find across both islands is kapa making. Kapa, or bark cloth, is crafted from the inner bark of the wauke (paper mulberry) tree. The process is labor-intensive—harvesting, soaking, pounding, and dyeing the cloth using natural pigments from local plants. Patterns are pressed in with bamboo stamps, often telling stories of the land, family lineage, or spiritual beliefs.

Another ancient practice still alive today is lauhala weaving. The word "lauhala" refers to the leaves of the hala tree, which are carefully dried and woven into mats, hats, baskets, and bracelets. If you stop by a community fair or visit a local craft co-op, chances are you'll meet a weaver who's been practicing since childhood, likely taught by a grandmother or auntie. The artistry lies not just in the technique but in the patience and presence required to create something both useful and beautiful.

Both kapa and lauhala are more than decorative—they're practical, symbolic, and deeply rooted in Hawaiian identity. In recent years, there's been a resurgence in learning and teaching these skills, not for tourists, but to ensure younger generations don't lose the knowledge that was nearly erased by colonization and commercialization.

Communities That Keep Culture Alive

While you might find upscale art galleries in parts of Hawaii, Molokai and Lanai are home to something arguably more powerful: artisan communities that practice their crafts in ways that are grounded, communal, and culturally meaningful.

On Molokai, the Saturday farmers market in Kaunakakai is more than a place to buy produce. It's where you'll meet painters, carvers, lei makers, and storytellers who gather not only to sell their wares but to connect with neighbors and visitors alike. You'll hear music playing, see families stopping by with their dogs, and smell the fragrance of freshly made plumeria leis. Ask a vendor about their work, and you'll almost always hear a story—about how their grandmother made the same type of bracelet or why they chose that particular plant to make their natural dye.

Lanai has its own version of this slower, more intentional creative energy. Though smaller in scale, the local artist scene here is just as committed. Look for handcrafted goods at pop-up stands, cultural events, or small boutique stores in Lanai City. Many of the artists are also educators, offering workshops in weaving or hula implements, especially during local festivals or cultural heritage weeks.

Art as Expression and Legacy

Across both islands, art is often used as a form of storytelling—preserving legends, honoring ancestors, and expressing contemporary challenges. Murals on the sides of community buildings might depict a historical moment or honor a revered local figure. Sculptures carved from koa wood or lava rock often reflect ancient myths or symbolic values, like balance, protection, or unity.

Even tattoos—called kakau—carry this same cultural weight. Traditional Hawaiian tattoos often represent genealogy, social status, or protection. While not as publicly visible due to the private nature of the practice, many locals still carry ancestral designs that have been passed down and carefully adapted by modern practitioners trained in traditional technique.

One of the most compelling examples of artistic legacy can be found in the public library or cultural centers, where exhibitions often feature youth projects in traditional forms. These programs are designed not only to preserve the techniques but also to help young people build a stronger sense of identity. You're not just looking at a craft—you're seeing someone reconnect with where they came from.

Engaging With Art as a Visitor

You don't need to be an artist to participate. In fact, some of the most rewarding experiences are hands-on. Both Molokai and Lanai offer opportunities to try your hand at traditional crafts, especially if you plan your visit around community events. Look for lei-making workshops, lauhala bracelet classes, or kapa demonstrations at local cultural centers. These are typically hosted by local practitioners who walk you through the meaning and the process—not just the technique.

If you're more of an observer than a maker, visiting local galleries, outdoor installations, and artisan markets still offers a rich experience. Many of these artists sell work directly from their homes or small, cooperative storefronts, where purchases directly support local families. You're not just buying a souvenir—you're helping to keep a tradition alive.

A Brushstroke of Memory

While on Lanai, I joined a small lei-making workshop held behind a community center. There were five of us sitting under a tree, listening to slack key guitar on a portable speaker while Auntie Nalani taught us how to twist and loop the ti leaves. Her fingers moved with practiced grace while mine stumbled, but she laughed gently and adjusted my technique.

As we worked, she told us how she learned the skill from her mother, who had learned from hers, and how each lei made for a wedding, a funeral, or a school graduation was a way of passing love through the hands. By the end, my lei was uneven but intact—and something I was proud to wear for the rest of the day.

It wasn't about making something perfect. It was about participating, listening, and being part of something that had been going on for generations. That single hour taught me more about Hawaiian culture than a full week of sightseeing ever could.

Local Language and Common Phrases

Language isn't just about communication—it's about connection. On Lanai and Molokai, where tradition is deeply rooted and community ties run strong, even a few simple Hawaiian words can open doors to more meaningful conversations, smiles, and invitations. While you'll find that English is widely spoken, learning basic 'ōlelo Hawai'i (the Hawaiian language) is one of the most respectful and rewarding ways to deepen your experience.

The Language That Almost Disappeared

It's important to understand the context before diving into vocabulary. Hawaiian isn't just a local accent—it's a language with deep historical, spiritual, and cultural significance. For much of the 20th century, it was at risk of vanishing altogether. After the overthrow of the Hawaiian Kingdom in 1893, the language was banned in schools and suppressed in public life. For decades, children were punished for speaking it, and as a result, fewer families passed it on to future generations.

But that tide has turned. Thanks to dedicated language revitalization efforts—many led by grassroots organizations on Molokai and other neighbor islands—'ōlelo Hawai'i is making a powerful comeback. Immersion schools, cultural programs, and local media now support its use in everyday life. When you visit, you're stepping into a place where language is more than just sound. Its identity, its resistance, and its pride.

Words You'll Hear Often

Even if you don't speak Hawaiian fluently, you'll quickly become familiar with a handful of words and phrases that show up everywhere—from road signs to restaurant menus to casual conversation. Here are a few you'll hear often and can comfortably use during your travels:

Aloha—this is more than just "hello" or "goodbye." Aloha is a way of being. It conveys love, compassion, respect, and harmony. When you say it, mean it.

Mahalo—thank you. You'll see it on trash cans, receipts, and signs, but it's best when said face-to-face. "Mahalo nui loa" means "thank you very much."

'Ohana—family. But it doesn't just mean blood relatives—it's the community you belong to, the people you take care of, and who take care of you.

Keiki—children. You'll hear it at beaches, restaurants, and parks when referencing little ones.

Wahine / Kāne – Woman / Man. Useful for restrooms and respectful language.

Pono—A sense of righteousness, balance, and moral responsibility. You'll hear it in phrases like "live pono," encouraging people to act with integrity.

Many locals will appreciate your effort, even if your pronunciation isn't perfect. And when in doubt, just ask. Most people are happy to help you learn.

Essential Phrases for Travelers

A few simple expressions can go a long way when you're exploring the islands:

E komo mai—Welcome. Often seen at the entrances to homes, shops, and festivals.

Pehea 'oe? – How are you? (Pronounced: peh-heh-ah oh-eh)

Maika'i au— I'm good/well. (Pronounced: mah-ee-kah-ee ow)

A'ole pilikia— No problem / You're welcome. A kind reply to "mahalo."

'Ae / 'A'ole – Yes / No

Even just using "aloha" and "mahalo" with intention creates a better exchange. Locals often note when a visitor takes the time to say a few words in Hawaiian—it shows respect for the place and the people.

Why Language Matters Here

For Native Hawaiians, language is more than vocabulary—it's a vessel for tradition, storytelling, and spirituality. Many chants, prayers, and songs don't have direct English equivalents, and much of their meaning is tied to rhythm, tone, and poetic structure.

Stories passed down through generations—moʻolelo—often rely on double meanings and layered metaphors. A chant about the wind might also be about a lover, a battle, or a journey. To understand the Hawaiian language is to unlock those stories, even if just in fragments.

When travelers engage with the language, even in small ways, they're participating in cultural preservation. You become part of the effort to keep ʻōlelo Hawaiʻi alive—not as a tourist curiosity, but as a living, evolving part of daily life.

How to Learn More While You're Here

If the language piques your interest—and for many travelers it does—there are plenty of ways to go deeper:

Community centers on both islands occasionally offer beginner-level classes, especially around cultural festivals or events. Some local museums or heritage centers have interactive exhibits where you can listen to native speakers or learn pronunciation basics.

Popular apps like Duolingo or ʻŌlelo Online offer lessons in Hawaiian language and are a great tool to start practicing before your trip or while winding down in the evening. Ask your local hosts, tour guides, or shopkeepers to teach you a word or two—it's often the start of a great conversation.

You might not leave fluent, but you'll leave with more than just vocabulary—you'll carry the beginning of a new understanding.

A Moment of Language, A Moment of Connection

During a visit to a Saturday market on Molokai, I stopped at a stand selling taro chips and noticed a small sign that read, "Mahalo for supporting our 'ohana farm." I said "mahalo" back as I paid, and the vendor—a woman in her sixties—smiled and said, "You get the accent pretty good. Not many try."

We ended up chatting for ten minutes. She told me about how her parents used to farm taro in the valleys near Halawa, how they spoke Hawaiian at home when she was young, and how she was teaching her grandkids the language now, "so they don't forget who they are."

That one word—mahalo—opened the door to a conversation I'll never forget. Sometimes, that's all it takes.

Connecting with Locals—Insider Tips

Most people who visited Lanai or Molokai remember their trip because of meaningful interactions with residents during meals or shared laughter. That's the heartbeat of these islands—its people. The people who call this place home actively create visitor experiences that are unique and cannot be replicated by any printed tour guide or scheduled plan. Openness, humility, and genuine respect serve as the foundation for building meaningful connections.

Start With Presence, Not Performance

Although fluency in Hawaiian and deep cultural knowledge can enhance your experience, they are not prerequisites for building genuine connections with local residents. Your presence takes precedence over your performance. Are you listening more than you're speaking? Do your questions emerge from genuine curiosity rather than anticipated answers? Visitors who display authenticity can easily be recognized by people on Molokai and Lanai, who warmly welcome those who engage instead of consuming.

It helps to slow down. Avoid a quick pass through stores and stay a moment at fruit stands on the side of the road. Take a moment. Take a moment to inquire about the vendor's daily experience. Show appreciation of the hand-carved kukui nut necklace or ask the vendor about the ingredients in their lilikoi jam. These brief interactions may lead to deeper connections.

Where and How to Engage

You will have better opportunities to form meaningful connections with people when you visit places where locals regularly meet. The occasion could be any local community event, including beach cleanups or cultural festivals, along with craft fairs. These venues naturally foster interaction since all attendees share a common goal.

Volunteer opportunities are another excellent entry point. Through your participation in a local conservation effort or taro patch assistance, you support the land and connect directly with its caretakers. When you join others in planting together or share a meal afterward, conversations unfold without effort.

Even everyday interactions offer chances to connect. Favor small family-run businesses where the owner simultaneously serves as the server or creator. Engage locals by asking about their life stories with true curiosity instead of hunting for a tourist photo opportunity.

Lead With Respect and Humility

Kuleana stands as the fundamental principle that dictates respectful interactions in Hawaii through its emphasis on both personal and collective responsibility. Your interaction with people here transports you into a cultural realm founded on historical generations of endurance. Humility is the most important quality you should bring.

That means being mindful of boundaries. Each conversation won't necessarily result in an invitation. There are sound reasons behind why some locals prefer to keep their cultural heritage private or guarded. Patience and a lack of entitlement during your interactions lead to meaningful differences. A cultural experience should not be expected, but when received, it becomes a precious gift.

Respecting local customs and rhythms becomes essential when you visit. You should not take pictures during a hula performance because it interrupts the act. Don't treat sacred sites like playgrounds. Avoid thinking you possess superior knowledge compared to the local residents. The actions are basic, yet they create a significant positive impact.

Guides Who Bring Stories to Life

Hiring a local guide is one of the smartest and most enriching decisions you can make while visiting. These guides don't just recite facts—they bring the land and culture to life through personal stories, ancestral knowledge, and lived experience.

You might hike a lesser-known trail on Lanai with someone whose grandparents once tended goats there. Or snorkel off the coast of Molokai while hearing legends tied to the reef. These aren't scripted tours—they're conversations shaped by the moment, the tide, and the energy of the day.

Many guides offer small-group or private options, which create a more intimate setting for questions, reflections, and stories to unfold. If you're lucky, you might find yourself sharing a meal or being introduced to other members of the guide's community. These are the kinds of moments that travelers remember for years to come—not because they were dramatic, but because they were real.

Stories That Leave a Mark

One afternoon on Lanai, I joined a small hiking group led by a local named Malia. The trail wove through kiawe trees and dusty hills, eventually opening up to a ridge with views of neighboring islands. As we rested, she told us about growing up nearby, how her uncle used to bring her to this spot to pick medicinal herbs and talk story.

Then she paused and added, "When I bring people here, I'm not just guiding them on a hike. I'm introducing them to my childhood."

There was a silence afterward—the good kind, when everyone is fully present. That's what these islands offer when you show up the right way. Not just photos and facts, but moments of shared humanity. And those don't fade when the trip ends.

You Carry What You Learn

The connections you make here may not always be loud or obvious. Sometimes they're a smile from the same barista each morning. Other times, they're a long conversation on a ferry ride. Whatever shape they take, they deepen your understanding of the place.

And here's the best part—when you return home, you carry those lessons with you. Maybe you slow down a bit more. Maybe you greet people more intentionally. Maybe you remember that kuleana doesn't end with vacation.

Because cultural immersion isn't about dipping your toes into someone else's world—it's about allowing it to change how you move in your own.

Chapter Five

Planning Your Itinerary

Adventure-Packed Weekends

Not everyone has two weeks to wander—sometimes, a weekend is all you've got. But even with just two days, Lanai and Molokai offer more than a taste of adventure. With the right planning and a willingness to rise with the sun, you can fit in everything from high-elevation hikes to ocean swims and still leave time to watch it all settle under a golden sky.

These aren't places where you check things off a list. They're places where even a short trip can feel full—because every experience connects you more deeply to the land, the water, and the quiet pulse of the islands.

Day One: Land-Based Adventure

Morning: Hiking the Munro Trail

Start early. The Munro Trail is one of Lanai's most scenic and rewarding hikes, and tackling it in the cool morning air makes a world of difference. The trail begins just above Lanai City and winds through Cook pine forests and upland ridges, offering sweeping views of neighboring islands and the island's own diverse terrain.

It's not a casual stroll—expect elevation changes, exposed stretches, and spots that require steady footing—but the reward is panoramic: distant coastlines, misty valleys, and, if you're lucky, a clear view of Molokai, Maui, and even the Big Island from a single vantage point.

Bring plenty of water, sturdy shoes, and layers. The weather can shift as you ascend, and sections of the trail can get muddy after rain. Download an offline map or go with a local guide who knows the trail's rhythms. They'll help you understand not just where you are, but what you're seeing.

Midday: Lunch in Lanai City

After your hike, head into Lanai City for a well-earned meal. Try a local café serving fresh poke bowls or a hearty plate lunch with island-raised beef. This is a good moment to slow down and take in the feel of the town—small, welcoming, and always a little cooler than the coast thanks to its elevation.

Afternoon: Off-Road Exploration by ATV

With the sun high and the energy flowing, trade boots for wheels and head off the beaten path. Several outfitters on Lanai offer ATV rentals or guided off-road tours that take you into rugged, less-traveled parts of the island. Trails lead to places like Keahiakawelo (Garden of the Gods), where the red rock formations glow in late-day light, or down dusty roads toward Shipwreck Beach, where a World War II-era tanker rusts offshore like a monument to another era.

The ride isn't just fun—it's a sensory overload. The smell of dry earth, the grit of wind-blown sand, and the unexpected silence of vast, open space all combine to make it unforgettable.

Evening: Sunset Picnic

Wrap the day with a simple picnic at Hulopoe Bay. Pick up local fruit, snacks, and maybe a bottle of wine or sparkling water, and settle into the sand as the sun sinks low. If you're staying nearby, you'll be able to walk back under the stars. If not, give yourself plenty of time to navigate after dark—rural roads can be winding and unlit.

Day Two: Water-Based Discovery

Morning: Snorkeling at Kepuhi Beach

Begin day two with a ferry ride or early wake-up on Molokai, and head straight to Kepuhi Beach for a morning snorkel. The beach is typically quiet, and the water, especially early in the day, is calm and clear. Vibrant coral reefs stretch just offshore, home to tropical fish, sea cucumbers, and the occasional sea turtle drifting through like a local with no appointments.

The key to a great snorkel here is minimal impact. Wear reef-safe sunscreen, avoid touching or standing on coral, and observe marine life from a respectful distance. It's not a zoo—it's a living system, and you're a guest.

Midday: Kayaking the Coastline

If conditions allow, rent a kayak or join a guided paddle along Molokai's shoreline. Some routes pass by ancient fishponds, coastal cliffs, and hidden coves, giving you a view of the island that few get to experience. Guides often share the history of these areas—stories of families who built the fishpond walls by hand or legends about the rock formations rising from the sea.

Even if you're not an experienced kayaker, the calm conditions near shore make this accessible. Just be sure to check tides and weather before launching.

Afternoon: Local Culture and Cooldown

Spend your final hours soaking up something that doesn't require movement: community. Stop at a local café or outdoor food stand. Walk through a farmers market if one's happening. Talk to someone. On Molokai, time slows down, and people still make eye contact. Let yourself match the pace.

Evening: Open Sky and Reflection

If your schedule allows, end your trip under the stars. Both Lanai and Molokai are excellent for stargazing thanks to minimal light pollution. Find an open field or coastal bluff and look up. You'll likely see more than just constellations—you'll feel the shift that happens when your body finally catches up with your surroundings.

Even a weekend here can do that. Not because you packed it full, but because you let the land speak. You showed up with intention, and the islands met you halfway.

Relaxation Retreats—Balancing Adventure and Downtime

Not all travel is meant to be packed. Sometimes the greatest luxury is unstructured time, especially on islands like Lanai and Molokai, where silence is still easy to find. A three-day retreat here isn't about doing less—it's about doing differently. With open mornings, gentle activities, and moments built around presence rather than productivity, this kind of itinerary leaves you rested, not rushed.

Day One: Ease Into Island Time

Morning: Gentle Arrival and Beach Yoga

Begin your retreat with a soft landing. Choose a coastal accommodation with easy beach access—Hulopoe Bay on Lanai or a quiet shoreline inn on Molokai's east side. Many eco-lodges and wellness-focused stays offer outdoor yoga classes or self-guided movement decks overlooking the ocean. There's no better way to shake off travel fatigue than stretching into a sun salutation while waves roll in nearby.

If yoga isn't your rhythm, just take a walk. The early light along these coastlines brings stillness and a sense of starting fresh.

Afternoon: Local Lunch and Light Exploration

Keep your afternoon light. Visit a local café for something nourishing—perhaps a grilled fish sandwich or a salad with fresh local greens. Afterward, explore slowly. Consider a stroll through Lanai City's quiet streets or Molokai's small community centers. Stop in a gallery or market. Let the day guide you instead of the clock.

Evening: Sunset Meditation or Spa Treatment

As the sun dips, give yourself space to transition gently into the evening. Many resorts offer spa services focused on traditional Hawaiian healing practices, such as lomilomi massage or herbal body treatments. If that's not available, find a bluff or a beach to sit quietly. Watch the colors shift. Listen. Let it be enough.

Day Two: Nourishment for Body and Mind

Morning: Visit a Botanical Garden or Cultural Site

Start the day with something rooted—literally. On Molokai, explore one of the restored *lo'i kalo* (taro patches) or guided garden tours that blend plants with stories. On Lanai, visit the Kanepuu Preserve, where native dryland forests reveal the beauty of the island's rare ecosystems.

These places aren't crowded, and they aren't loud. They invite learning at a different pace—one where observation is the lesson.

Afternoon: Guided Meditation or Creative Workshop

Some accommodations and community spaces offer guided meditation sessions, breathwork classes, or cultural workshops in lei-making or lauhala weaving. These experiences are hands-on without being strenuous, offering quiet engagement that centers the spirit while honoring local knowledge.

You'll leave with more than a souvenir—you'll carry a practice.

Evening: Farm-to-Table Dining

End the day with a meal that reflects the island's natural rhythm. Seek out restaurants that work with local farmers and fishermen. These places usually feature smaller menus, rotating with what's fresh and in season.

Meals tend to be slow-paced here, and that's the point. Stay awhile. Eat with intention. Taste what the land and sea have offered, and know you're part of a cycle that respects both.

Day Three: Rest, Reflect, and Reset

Morning: Solo Time in Nature

Your final morning should be yours entirely. Find a quiet path, a patch of sand, or a shaded grove. Leave the phone behind. Walk or sit without a destination. These are the kinds of moments that linger long after the flight home—when you remember how still you were and how full that stillness felt.

Afternoon: Writing, Reading, or Doing Nothing at All

Build space into your itinerary to do nothing—on purpose. Whether it's journaling in a hammock or finishing a novel by the sea, allow your mind to wander without guilt. The retreat isn't about activities. It's about permission to be.

Evening: Gentle Transition

As your time winds down, don't try to squeeze in one last outing. Instead, revisit a favorite spot from earlier in the trip. Sit in the same place. Notice what feels different. That's the gift of unhurried travel—you change while standing still.

Tips for a Stress-Free Experience

Don't over-plan: choose one or two activities per day, and let the rest unfold.

Leave space between experiences. Transition slowly, even between meals and rest.

Stay connected to the setting: Choose lodging that opens to nature, where windows bring in the breeze and outdoor spaces invite you to linger.

Honor your energy: If you feel like skipping something, skip it. The itinerary is a guide—not a requirement.

This kind of retreat doesn't require luxury. It requires intention. And in Lanai and Molokai, where the pace is already slower, you're in the perfect place to remember that rest is not a reward—it's part of the journey.

Cultural Explorations—A Two-Week Journey

Culture isn't something you absorb quickly. This cultural phenomenon becomes familiar by gradually living with it through repeated conversations and careful observation. A two-week journey gives travelers the opportunity to both witness and actively engage with local culture. Residents of Lanai and Molokai live their traditions daily rather than showcasing them for tourists, which creates opportunities to join island life through humility and openness the longer you stay.

This journey isn't about sightseeing. It's about immersion.

Week One: Foundations and Familiarization

Day 1–2: Arrival and Orientation

Begin on Lanai. Find time to adapt to both the new location and its unique rhythm. Explore Lanai City through a walking tour followed by a museum visit, and check out local shops and art galleries. Early cultural understanding often begins with simple conversations: a person describes the origin of their fish or the type of flower they included in their lei.

Day 3: Historical Sites and Storytelling

Come see Keahiakawelo (Garden of the Gods), where geological marvels meet legendary stories. A local guide will take you through the area while explaining the historical stories connected to the stones and terrain. Next stop is Kaunolu Village, which served as both a fishing community and a retreat for Hawaiian royalty. Visitors see more than just beautiful views because these locations hold historical memories.

Day 4–5: Molokai's Living Traditions

You can reach Molokai by traveling across water on a ferry or by flying on a small aircraft. Start your exploration with a guided tour of a restored loʻi kalo (taro patch) located in either Halawa Valley or Central Molokai. Join local families who have tended this land for generations to plant, harvest, or clean taro in their fields. While participating in tasks, it is essential to observe how local traditions and environmental factors determine each step.

Day 6–7: Cultural Events and Community Gatherings

Time permitting, coordinate your schedule with local events like Molokai's Ka Hula Piko festival or weekend farmers' markets, which feature live music and cultural demonstrations. You can find chances to participate in public luaus or church potlucks and storytelling circles outside of official events, which create a family reunion atmosphere rather than tourist attractions.

Enter the experience with an open heart without bringing your camera along. Your purpose is to form connections rather than capture moments.

Week Two: Participation and Personal Discovery

Day 8–9: Hands-On Learning

Select a traditional art form or practice to study in greater depth. Attend a lei-making workshop conducted by an artist from the community. Explore lauhala weaving techniques or understand the steps in kapa cloth production. Sit with a kumu who will teach you about the chants and lineages alongside the meanings of your practice instead of how to perform it.

These aren't crafts. They are languages without words. When you participate, you show respect for the culture.

Day 10–11: Culinary Connection

Approach food through the lens of practice instead of seeing it as a mere product. Enroll in a cooking course where you can prepare traditional foods such as laulau and lomi salmon together with haupia. Ask about how the ingredients were sourced. Learn the rhythm of the preparation. Explore where your ingredients originate by visiting local farms and fishponds.

Eating at this place becomes a cultural ritual, particularly during shared meals. Find an informal communal setting where people talk across the table between meals.

Day 12: Sacred Sites and Spiritual Spaces

Commit one complete day to understanding sacred sites as well as spiritual protocols and the kapu system. Join a local cultural interpreter for a heiau visit or explore guided walks through spaces of multilayered ancestral significance. The profound silence at these sacred locations evokes a devotional sensation even for non-religious people.

You should maintain a quiet, humble, and alert presence when visiting sacred locations. These are not tourist destinations. They are places of living memory.

Day 13–14: Reflection and Return

During the final two days, focus on revisiting the experiences that touched you. Go back to your favorite viewpoint, revisit your storyteller shopkeeper, or explore again the silent trail where you strolled alone. During this period you should dedicate time to journal and sketch your experiences or simply sit with what you have absorbed in order to fully experience its essence.

When possible, express your thanks to someone who assisted you by sharing food or showing appreciation. Even a handwritten note matters. In Hawaii, relationships carry weight. A purposeful conclusion holds equal importance to starting with clear intentions.

Building In Flexibility

Maintain flexibility in your structured plan to accommodate unexpected invitations and weather changes, or follow internal guidance. Some of the most meaningful cultural experiences happen unplanned: A spontaneous conversation continues beyond its expected end, a neighbor extends an invitation to their home, and you discover an opportunity to assist with an unforeseen task.

Your visit to a place turns into an immersive experience within a dynamic cultural atmosphere. This kind of listening demands flexibility because it operates beyond regular schedules.

Customizing Your Itinerary—Flexibility and Flow

Every traveler who visits the islands brings uniquely different stories with them. Some come to reset. Others come to learn. Tourists often reach the islands feeling both curious and tired while remaining uncertain whether they prefer to explore their surroundings or take time to relax. A carefully planned itinerary is not meant to serve as an unchangeable script.

The naturally slower pace and land-and-weather-driven rhythms of Lanai and Molokai make flexibility essential. The islanders prefer spontaneous exploration and being present over meticulous planning.

An ideal itinerary should be responsive to both the surrounding environment and personal emotional states while remaining attentive to human connections.

Balancing Adventure, Culture, and Rest

During itinerary planning, prioritize maintaining energy levels rather than focusing solely on scheduled activities. After completing a tough hike or kayaking session during the day, make sure to follow it with a relaxing morning activity like writing by the beach or exploring nearby stores. Allocate time for quiet reflection the day after you spend several hours absorbing cultural knowledge.

You do not need to make a choice between pursuing adventure with cultural experiences or combining relaxation with learning opportunities. Blend them.

For example:

Start your morning with yoga or meditation at sunrise before embarking on a brief walk along the coast.

Join a taro farm workday or explore a cultural center during the afternoon and wrap up your day with a sunset picnic.

Start your day with an ATV tour before attending a lei-making class in the evening.

Every activity builds upon the previous one to produce an experience that feels complete yet remains calm.

Alternating Guided and Independent Exploration

Guided experiences provide greater depth when exploring places like heiau and fishponds or learning about native plants. Some activities reach their full potential when you explore them alone according to your own timing. Mix both into your schedule.

Start your day with stories from a local expert, then spend your afternoon exploring freely without any planned activities. You'll start to recognize the ample room available for structured activities as well as unexpected events.

Embracing the Unplanned

Avoid scheduling every available slot in your calendar. Let your itinerary breathe. Leave entire mornings or afternoons unscheduled. Maintaining flexible time enables you to join community events or discover hidden beaches while providing space for rest when needed.

The best travel experiences occur unexpectedly because you allowed yourself the flexibility to accept them when they emerged.

Allow for Weather and Mood

On islands like these, weather shifts quickly. Rainstorms may arrive unexpectedly while ocean tides change positions and hiking trails get slippery. Instead of frustration, see it as an invitation to pivot, adapt, and explore something else.

The same goes for your energy. If you initially planned a hike but you find yourself wanting to be still, pay attention to it. When your interest leans towards a museum rather than snorkeling, choose the museum visit.

Your travel experience becomes transformative when you allow yourself to be shaped by it instead of forcing every event to fit your preconceived notions.

Tools to Help You Adapt

Offline planning apps, along with downloadable maps and hand-drawn guides obtained from local shops, enable navigation when internet service is unavailable. Outdoor explorers find useful data when using navigation applications such as Gaia GPS, AllTrails, and offline Google Maps for hiking trails and remote roads.

Daily and weekly event schedules can be obtained from community centers and visitor bureaus, which focus on pop-up markets, local festivals, and volunteering activities.

Community members typically possess more knowledge than any digital application can provide. Don't hesitate to ask for recommendations. When asking locals about the best time to visit a beach or the trail safety on any specific day, you will receive thoughtful responses, which often come with interesting stories.

Travel as Dialogue

You don't have to have a precisely scheduled itinerary when visiting Lanai and Molokai. It needs to be attuned. The most successful travel plans feel dynamic because they adapt to the islands and their people while listening to your inner voice, which urges you to either explore further or experience something different.

Build your schedule like you would a good conversation: The best travel schedules include listening space and surprise opportunities along with time for meaningful connections.

Travel here means not only visiting destinations but also allowing the environment to mold your movement patterns.

Designing a Journey That Fits You

Your itinerary design becomes a reflection of your personal values when it effectively guides your movement. The itinerary allows room for spontaneous moments, quiet time, and experiences without labels. The slower daily rhythms and strong cultural ties to land and community in Lanai and Molokai mean that time management focuses on meaningful activities rather than quantity.

When you engage fully with your moments, you discover how weekends can become extraordinary. You experience restoration when you rest for a few days and release your obligations. Two weeks of cultural immersion create memories that transform you beyond what you knew.

An itinerary truly works best when it mimics a dialogue with the destination. Between you and the land. The journey begins with your intentions but develops through the spontaneous invitations that emerge during your travels.

Make your plans with attention to detail before proceeding with openness. Allow your journey to reveal itself gradually through genuine moments, just as the islands naturally reveal themselves.

Chapter Six

Outdoor Adventures

There's a certain clarity that comes when your feet hit red dirt and the wind carries the scent of ironwood and eucalyptus. Lanai's hiking trails aren't just scenic—they're soul-resetting. Unlike the orchestrated experiences on more commercialized islands, the trails here feel raw, unfiltered, and deeply personal. You won't find crowds jostling for the perfect photo or vendors selling bottled water at the trailhead. What you will find are sweeping views, silent forests, and an open invitation to slow down and feel small in the best possible way.

The Munro Trail is where most adventures begin—and for good reason. It carves its way through the highlands of the island, offering panoramic views that stretch from Lanai to Molokai, Maui, and even the Big Island on a clear day.

The trail starts just above Lanai City and climbs steadily, weaving through Cook pine forests and mountain ridges. It's not a quick loop—it's a full-day commitment if you're doing it end to end—but every step feels worth it. This is the kind of trail where silence speaks louder than words, and moments of stillness catch you off guard in the best way.

A bit more accessible but no less spectacular is the Koloiki Ridge Trail. This one begins at the edge of the Four Seasons Resort Lanai, but don't let the luxury address fool you—the trail itself is pure nature. It winds through native forests, shaded by kukui and hala trees, and opens onto a ridgeline with views that make you stop in your tracks.

From the overlook, the Pacific unfolds below like a living canvas, and on the clearest days, you can trace the silhouette of Molokai across the water. It's the kind of place that makes you breathe differently—deeper, slower, more intentionally.

But what truly sets Lanai's hikes apart is the terrain itself. You're not just walking through landscapes—you're walking through stories. Take Keahiakawelo, better known as the Garden of the Gods. Located at the end of a rugged dirt road on the island's northwestern edge, it feels more Martian than Hawaiian.

Massive boulders are scattered across the landscape like they were tossed there by giants. The soil glows a rusty red, especially at sunset, when the entire scene looks like it's been lit from within. According to local legend, the land was shaped by a spiritual battle between kahuna (priests) from Lanai and Molokai. Whether you believe in myths or not, it's hard to stand there and not feel like something powerful happened.

Closer to the coast, volcanic rock formations rise like ancient monuments along the shoreline. These jagged outcrops, worn by salt and time, speak to the island's fiery origins and ongoing transformation. There's a stark beauty in their solitude—unpolished, enduring, and humbling.

Before you lace up your hiking boots, though, a few words of preparation. Lanai's trails are as wild as they are rewarding. Hydration is non-negotiable—bring more water than you think you'll need, especially during dry seasons when shade is scarce. Sun protection is equally critical; the sun doesn't play favorites here, and even forested paths offer only intermittent cover. Cell service is spotty at best, so having a GPS-enabled map downloaded ahead of time can be a lifesaver—literally.

And as you step onto the trail, remember this: you're a guest in a living landscape. The land here breathes its own rhythm, one shaped by centuries of wind, water, and reverence. Practice the Leave No Trace principles—take nothing, leave nothing. Stay on marked paths, resist the urge to shortcut switchbacks, and tread lightly. Wildlife here may be elusive, but it's present. Give it space. Notice its patterns. You're not just observing—you're participating.

Lanai doesn't try to impress you with spectacle. It impresses with its presence. The trails ask you to meet them with the same intention—with open eyes, a quiet mind, and a heart ready for stillness.

Snorkeling in Molokai's Pristine Waters

The ocean off Molokai doesn't just invite you in—it humbles you. It's not loud with motorboats or lined with beach bars. It's calm, expansive, and alive in a way that asks you to listen before you leap. Snorkeling here is less about thrill and more about presence. You float, you watch, you breathe. And in return, the sea opens up its secrets.

One of the most accessible and rewarding spots is Kepuhi Beach on Molokai's west side. The shoreline curves gently, and just offshore, vibrant coral gardens stretch below the surface like underwater meadows. Here, colorful fish weave through coral towers while sea cucumbers and urchins anchor themselves in the sand. On calm mornings, the visibility is so clear you'll feel like you're gliding over glass. It's the kind of place where a quiet hour can feel like a deep meditation.

A short distance away is Turtle Town, a lesser-known gem with a name that says it all. Green sea turtles, or honu, glide gracefully through these waters, often surfacing within arm's reach—though it's crucial to admire from a respectful distance. They are not pets or props but ancient navigators of this coastline. Watching one up close is like witnessing a moving prayer: slow, deliberate, and strangely profound.

Molokai's marine life tells its own story. Schools of yellow tang shimmer like underwater sunbursts, while butterflyfish dart through coral crevices in synchronized movement. If you're lucky—and quiet—you might spot a spotted eagle ray coasting by or even a monk seal resting on a distant rock shelf. These moments don't feel orchestrated. They feel earned.

But this underwater beauty is also fragile. Coral reefs here aren't just scenery; they're living systems, centuries in the making, and easily damaged by careless touch. That's why preparing properly matters. Before you head out, make sure your gear fits well and is reef-safe—literally. Fins should be soft-edged and controlled, not churning up sediment or scraping coral heads. Your sunscreen? Make it reef-safe, without oxybenzone or other reef-harming chemicals. A small choice, but one that echoes loudest underwater.

Tides here shift with quiet power, and currents can surprise even strong swimmers. Always check local tide schedules and weather conditions before heading out. If you're unfamiliar with the area, local guides are more than happy to share not just safe access points, but stories about the water you're about to enter—myths, customs, and history passed down like oral charts. And bring the basics: a well-fitted mask, snorkel, and a dry bag for essentials. Respect the ocean by being prepared.

The ocean here doesn't ask for performance. You don't need to dive deep or chase after anything. Just float. Just watch. Let the rhythm of the reef recalibrate your own. The longer you stay still, the more life reveals itself.

Snorkeling on Molokai isn't about collecting photos—it's about participating in something ancient and alive. The more gently you move, the more you'll see. And long after your gear is packed away, the quiet of that underwater world stays with you. It whispers a little slower, a little deeper—just like Molokai itself.

Off the Beaten Path: Hidden Trails and Secret Spots

Some places don't appear on maps. They're marked instead by the shift in wind, the quiet curve of a hidden footpath, or the rustle of leaves just off the main trail. On Lanai and Molokai, these kinds of places exist in abundance—quiet, sacred, and often overlooked. If you're willing to step away from the expected, you'll find that some of the islands' most unforgettable moments lie just beyond the guidebook.

On Lanai, a narrow trail leads through kiawe trees toward Halulu Heiau, a centuries-old Hawaiian temple nestled in silence. It's not obvious at first. There are no signs or crowded trailheads. But if you follow the path—sometimes more intuition than instruction—you'll arrive at a stone structure tucked into the hillside, framed by wild grasses and open sky. The heiau is humble in form but vast in presence. It asks for reverence, not explanation. There's no plaque to tell you what to feel. You just feel it.

Then there are the cliffside trails that trace Lanai's northern shoreline—paths that rarely see more than a few footprints in a day. These routes reveal panoramic views of the Pacific that stretch endlessly, interrupted only by seabirds and the occasional spray of distant surf.

There's one spot, just past an old cattle gate, where the cliffs drop away and you feel, quite suddenly, like you're standing on the edge of the world. It's not dangerous if you tread carefully—but it does remind you that wildness still exists and that it's something to approach with respect.

On Molokai, the secrets lie deeper in the valleys and behind the waterfalls. Hidden among the dense forests are falls that don't have names on maps but live in local memory. Some require a local guide—both for navigation and for understanding their significance. These are not places to "conquer" or "check off." They're places to enter gently, with listening as your first act.

One such trail leads to a secluded bay only accessible by foot. The sand is coarse, the waves powerful, and more often than not, you'll be the only one there. Bring what you need and leave no trace behind—not just because it's right, but because it's the kind of place that makes you want to tread softly, instinctively.

Discovering these spots safely requires more than curiosity—it requires preparation and humility. Local guides are often your best asset, not just for finding the trails but for understanding them. They'll tell you which trails flood quickly, where native birds nest, and which stones are more than just rocks—they're altars, markers, or resting places. If you're exploring solo, take a physical map and learn to read local trail markers, many of which are subtle—stacked stones, changes in vegetation, or wooden signs weathered by salt and time.

Every island has its secrets. But Lanai and Molokai don't guard theirs with fences—they simply wait. And when you do find these places, they don't scream for attention. They whisper. And if you listen closely, you'll return not with stories of what you saw, but of what you felt.

These trails don't promise ease—they offer honesty. They'll challenge your legs, ask for your patience, and reward you with a deeper sense of connection. The kind you can't photograph. The kind you carry home in the silence between your thoughts.

Eco-Friendly Adventures: Respecting the Land

You can create unforgettable experiences on Lanai and Molokai without causing any environmental damage. The most profound experiences here are found in silent adventures that connect you to the land's natural pace instead of creating new paths. Exploration alongside preservation becomes evident when you visit these islands since they demonstrate how these two concepts work together.

Explore the Molokai coastline on a kayaking tour where narrow channels run between coral reefs while sea cliffs stand tall above the ocean surface. This area's finest tours focus on raising awareness rather than delivering adrenaline rushes. Conservation-focused local guides lead tours through the waterways and give insights into the historical past.

While paddling along, you will learn about Hawaiian ancestral fishpond engineering and discover the balance necessary for marine life survival. While you might see a couple of sea turtles during your visit, the key lesson is understanding how life prospers through silence, space, and care.

Guided eco-tours on Lanai offer travelers more than just traditional viewpoints. These are not sightseeing trips. They're education in motion. During the tour you could explore a reforestation project where indigenous plants are brought back to improve watershed health or examine a coastline where cleaning efforts and erosion studies take place.

Throughout this journey you'll be introduced to Hawaiian ahupuaʻa systems, which see the land as an interconnected living system extending from mountain ranges to ocean shores. This adventure presents a unique experience that moves the excitement from material acquisition to intellectual discovery.

The health of the land for future generations depends on the dedicated efforts of volunteers, researchers, and community members working behind the scenes. Across Molokai, marine conservation programs function through local efforts to monitor reef health together with the removal of invasive species.

The land-based conservation work protects rare bird species, restores wetland areas, and reconstructs habitats for native plant life. These aren't flashy initiatives. They're daily acts of care.

Visitors have the opportunity to participate in these activities.

While beach cleanups may not seem like traditional adventures, they become meaningful experiences when you join schoolchildren and community leaders to remove microplastics from the sand. It shifts your idea of impact.

Community-led environmental initiatives often possess quiet strength while maintaining an informal approach. When you ask people around you about local initiatives they participate in, you might receive an invitation to join them.

Getting involved with local conservation efforts doesn't require physical labor. Supporting local conservation efforts can involve staying at eco-friendly accommodations or making quiet donations to local organizations that carry out the work. You should ask your guide how they protect the places they show visitors and pick the ones who provide satisfactory answers.

A multitude of organizations provide public lectures and educational workshops for those who want to expand their knowledge. Educational topics include native plant propagation along with ocean stewardship and cultural land practices.

Certain tours incorporate these educational lessons into their itinerary, whereas others organize them as separate events. You should feel free to attend any available talks or workshops even if you are only visiting temporarily. The land remembers everyone who listens.

Exploration in this region requires humility rather than pursuing extreme activities. The right approach to paddling involves going around reefs rather than proceeding through them. In the questions you ask a guide. The decisions you make to leave no footprints behind define your relationship with the land.

Respect isn't an add-on—it's the foundation. The islands will share their finest tales when approached with proper care.

The Journey is the Invitation

The islands of Lanai and Molokai are destinations where fast-paced excitement is not the reason for travel. Your visit here delivers an experience that develops at a slower pace with greater authenticity. Adventure in this place does not depend on the number of meters climbed or social media popularity.

The true measure of adventure comes from the silent thrill of discovery. You suddenly become aware of the fact that you have been trekking for hours alone. The splash of color below sea level causes you to hold your breath. An unknown path reveals itself to be a journey that leads you back to your inner self.

The islands provide visitors with an intimate connection to the land rather than a simple list of activities. Every trail and hidden path, along with each reef, invites people to establish connections instead of exploiting resources. There's a kind of sacredness in that. Attention allows natural reverence to emerge instead of the land demanding respect.

Keep your gear minimal in your daypack and your outlook simple in your expectations. Bring curiosity. Leave assumptions. Approach your adventure with openness by allowing the island to determine your path rather than controlling it yourself. While exploring this area, your presence holds more value than your planned schedule.

When you come back with sand in your shoes and salt scent on your skin along with newfound quiet thoughts, then you know your travel was successful.

Chapter Seven

Navigating the Islands

Getting around Lanai and Molokai isn't just about movement—it's about immersion. On these islands, transportation doesn't exist to rush you from one photo op to the next. Instead, it helps you slow down and *feel* the rhythm of place. Whether you're tracing the curve of a coastline by car or pedaling through rustling groves of ironwood trees, every mode of travel offers a different window into island life.

Vehicle Rental

If you're looking to explore beyond the town centers or reach the more rugged corners of Lanai or Molokai, renting a vehicle gives you the most flexibility. But not all rentals are created equal here.

Rental Cars

Lanai, in particular, has long stretches of unpaved roads and off-road terrain, especially leading to places like Keahiakawelo (the Garden of the Gods) or Polihua Beach. If your journey takes you off the asphalt, you'll want a four-wheel-drive vehicle capable of handling red-dirt roads and steep inclines. Standard sedans might manage the paved paths, but they won't get you to the most remote and unforgettable spots.

On Molokai, road conditions are more forgiving, but a rental car is still your best bet for reaching places like the Halawa Valley or the cliff-top Kalaupapa Lookout. Vehicle availability can fluctuate based on the season, so it's wise to book in advance—especially if you're arriving with a plan in mind.

Even though driving here can feel refreshingly uncrowded, it comes with its own rhythm. Speed limits are low, and locals value patience and courtesy over urgency. You're not just passing through—you're participating in a lifestyle. Let the pace guide you.

Bikes and ATVs

For travelers craving a more tactile connection to the land, bikes and ATVs offer a different kind of freedom. In Lanai City or Molokai's town centers, bike rentals are often available for short excursions or full-day adventures. Cycling along the coast or through gently winding backroads puts you in direct touch with the landscape—you hear more, see more, and feel every shift in elevation beneath your tires.

If you're venturing off the beaten path, ATV rentals open the door to landscapes that cars can't comfortably reach. Remote trails and dusty ridgelines become accessible with a bit more horsepower. That said, this is not a place for speeding. Whether on two wheels or four, exploration is best done with a light footprint and a steady hand.

Public Transportation and Island Shuttles

Unlike more urban destinations, public transportation here is minimal—and that's part of the charm. On Molokai, a simple shuttle system connects key points like the airport, town, and some lodging areas. Routes and hours can be limited, so plan around availability rather than assuming constant service.

Lanai offers hotel-based shuttles that serve major stops, especially if you're staying at one of the island's primary resorts. These services are reliable for reaching beaches, trailheads, or returning from dinner in town—but again, schedules vary and are often aligned with hotel activity rather than a fixed timetable.

In both cases, don't expect a sprawling bus grid or rideshare availability. What you will find, however, is the opportunity to reconnect with the idea that travel doesn't need to be immediate—it just needs to be intentional.

Reading the Roads

Driving here is unlike driving anywhere else. Unpaved roads are common on Lanai, and even Molokai has routes that narrow unexpectedly or meander through quiet farmland. You won't find many street signs—and when you do, they often serve as gentle suggestions rather than strict instructions. Keep an eye out for roaming deer, wild turkeys, and sudden drop-offs where pavement gives way to dirt.

It's wise to check weather conditions before setting out, especially during the rainy season. A sunlit morning can shift quickly, and some roads become impassable in heavy rain. Having a printed or offline map on hand never hurts—cell service can fade the farther you get from town.

Driving here is less about convenience and more about curiosity. Each road has a personality. Some lead to known landmarks, others to unexpected moments of beauty you'll remember long after you've left the island.

Efficient Island Hopping — A Step-by-Step Guide

Island hopping in Hawaii isn't just about logistics—it's about **rhythm**. Each island has its own tempo, its own mood, its own lessons to teach. Moving between Lanai, Molokai, and their neighboring islands requires some planning, but it rewards you with an experience that feels like you're moving through chapters of a story rather than simply changing locations.

Ferries and Flights

There are no massive cruise ports or bustling international airports on Lanai and Molokai—just modest terminals and welcoming smiles. This limited access keeps things intimate and, sometimes, unpredictable.

Ferry services typically operate between Lanai and nearby islands like Maui, offering a scenic and straightforward journey across the water. These rides can be memorable in their own right—passing whales during the migration season, catching rainbows arcing over the sea, or watching distant islands rise out of morning mist. But schedules vary with the seasons and the weather, so checking availability in advance is key.

For those traveling to or from Molokai, small regional planes are the norm. These short flights connect to islands like Oahu and Maui, often departing from smaller commuter terminals. It's not the kind of flight with in-flight entertainment or meal service, but it's the kind where the pilot might greet you by name—and the windows offer postcard views the entire way.

From Island to Island with Intention

Island hopping isn't about squeezing more into your itinerary—it's about stretching your experience across landscapes and lifestyles that contrast and complement one another. With that in mind, it helps to plan each transition as a day in itself, not just a transfer.

Here's a simple rhythm that tends to work well:

Start Early: Morning crossings give you more flexibility and reduce the risk of weather-related delays.

Travel Light: Packing only what you need for the day allows easier movement through ferry docks and smaller planes with baggage restrictions.

Leave Room for Flexibility: Unexpected moments often define the journey—staying a little longer in a port town, exploring a café you hadn't planned on, or adjusting your route to chase a golden sunset.

Treat island hopping not as a task, but as a travel chapter—a bridge that connects not only destinations, but moods.

Mapping the Best Flow

When mapping out your journey, it's helpful to visualize the triangular relationship between Lanai, Molokai, and their neighboring islands. While you might start on Maui, hop to Lanai for seclusion, and then fly to Molokai for culture, each connection has its own ideal flow.

Some travelers choose to circle back to a larger hub island—like Maui or Oahu—for outbound flights. Others embrace the loop, beginning and ending in different places entirely. The right path depends on your pace and priorities.

If minimizing travel time is essential, aim for direct routes whenever possible, even if it means adjusting your itinerary slightly. But if you're open to slower transitions, the space between islands becomes part of the magic—those open water crossings and sky-bound shortcuts offer their own kind of beauty.

Tips for a Seamless Hop

Check the Forecast: Ocean crossings and small aircraft are both sensitive to weather. A quick check the night before can save hours the next day.

Confirm Luggage Limits: Especially on smaller planes, baggage restrictions can be tighter than you'd expect. Knowing the limits ahead of time prevents last-minute stress.

Keep Essentials Accessible: If your main bag ends up stowed or limited, having a small carry-on with your essentials (water, ID, sunscreen, etc.) will keep your day flowing smoothly.

Build in Breathing Room: Give yourself time between travel and activities. Let the pace of the islands guide your transitions rather than racing the clock.

The beauty of traveling between Lanai, Molokai, and their neighbors is that each movement feels deliberate. There's no rush, no crowds funneling you through terminals. Just the quiet unfolding of the next destination—and the anticipation of what you'll discover there.

Understanding Local Directions

Some directions come from satellites. Others come from the soul of the land.

In Hawaii, and especially on islands like Lanai and Molokai, navigation isn't just about roads and GPS—it's about orientation to nature. You won't always hear "north" or "south" when locals give directions. Instead, you'll hear something far more grounded: *mauka* and *makai*.

Mauka means "toward the mountains."

Makai means "toward the sea."

These words are more than directional cues. They reflect a way of life shaped by geography, by rhythm, by reverence. In ancient times, Hawaiians organized everything—from planting to prayer—based on their position relative to land and ocean. That instinct remains. It's how people think. How they live. And if you listen closely, it becomes a compass that connects you to something deeper.

Learning to Navigate Like a Local

You might hear someone say, "The beach is two blocks makai from the store," or "There's a trailhead just up mauka from the last house on the right." These aren't abstract directions—they're invitations to pay attention to your surroundings.

Where is the ocean? Where do the hills rise? You begin to notice the way the light falls differently facing the mountains. You begin to feel the temperature shift as you climb mauka, or hear the hush of waves draw you makai. These are land-based cues, and they give you more than guidance—they give you presence.

Even signs on some hiking trails or village paths might use these terms without explanation. But the beauty of *mauka* and *makai* is that they don't need translation once you understand them. You feel them in your bones. You follow them the way you follow the wind.

When Mauka and Makai Matter

Imagine this: You've just finished a quiet lunch in Lanai City. You ask a local where to find the nearest lookout point. They smile and say, "Take the road past the old post office, head mauka, and follow the bend." No map, no coordinates—just a natural reference to your orientation.

Or maybe you're in Molokai, walking near the coast. A vendor at the farmers market tells you the best taro patch views are a short walk "makai from the school." You turn toward the breeze, toward the sound of distant surf, and follow the direction that feels true.

These aren't tricks for navigation. They're cultural signposts. They help you move through the islands, not just across them.

Asking for Directions: An Invitation to Connect

In remote areas or smaller towns, formal signage may be sparse or weather-worn. That's when the best tool isn't your phone—it's your voice. Asking a local for directions becomes a shared moment. People here are often generous with their time and eager to help, especially when approached with respect.

If you're lucky, the answer might include a personal anecdote—"My uncle helped build that trail," or "That grove of trees marks an old gathering spot." Suddenly, you're not just getting directions. You're getting introduced to the island.

A Reflection of Respect

Understanding and using *mauka* and *makai* isn't about sounding local—it's about moving through Hawaii with awareness. It's about embracing a system of orientation that's not rooted in compasses, but in community. When you use these terms, you're not just navigating—you're participating in a worldview that honors the relationship between land and sea, human and horizon.

So as you make your way across Lanai and Molokai, pause now and then. Look mauka. Look makai. Let the mountains guide your back and the ocean draw you forward. The path may not always be marked, but it will always be there—waiting for you to find it, one quiet step at a time.

Remote Location Navigation — Maps and Apps

The best views in Lanai and Molokai can be discovered beyond paved roads and beyond the final road sign or through areas where cell signal disappears. The exploration process requires introspective awareness rather than confident forward momentum. Despite being equipped with GPS technology we use today, successful navigation requires travelers to combine readiness with modesty.

Tools for the Trail: Maps that Guide, Apps that Adapt

Remote areas of these islands experience unreliable connectivity at best. Deep inland trails and cliffside paths often suffer from non-existent or poor cell signal coverage. The lack of coverage is not a system failure but a fundamental part of the trail experience. By stepping away from the signal you enter a state of stillness.

Download offline maps before you leave to ensure safe and confident navigation during your trip. Multiple versatile mapping applications provide offline access features along with topographic overlays and trail tracking capabilities independent of network availability. Numerous mapping applications provide elevation indicators and location tagging functionality that proves helpful when exploring new environments. Make sure that you download and save your map files while you still have internet access.

Physical printed maps receive too little appreciation despite their old-fashioned nature. Hikers won't experience power losses or technical malfunctions when using physical trail maps during their journey. Paper maps at visitor centers and local shops contain handwritten notes and local shortcuts that provide insights which digital maps do not capture.

Challenges of Remote Navigation

There are some paths that have no labels. The Munro Trail on Lanai splits into small trails which are unmarked and not widely known. The thick vegetation in Molokai's central regions along with its coastal ridges hides trail signs while some areas completely lack signage. Total reliance on visual guidance becomes confusing when weather conditions change.

Weather conditions can change visibility quickly especially when mist descends or the sun disappears behind mountains sooner than you anticipate. Morning clarity can transform into dense fog that covers the view by afternoon.

Wayfinding here requires attention, not just equipment. Look for natural landmarks: Look for natural landmarks such as an ironwood tree stand beside a ridge curve while listening to ocean surf sounds reverberate through the valleys. Navigating becomes more relational than precise because it involves recognizing your placement in the world as an integral part of it rather than a separate entity.

Safe Exploration

Because short hikes or drives into the hills may lead to rapid isolation it is important to prepare carefully. Essentials include:

Always inform someone about your travel itinerary before undertaking any solo adventures or backcountry explorations.

Bring additional water supplies with snacks and sun protection because weather conditions and trail lengths can change unexpectedly.

Always bring a power bank or backup battery if your map system runs on a phone.

Include a first-aid kit, flashlight, and lightweight jacket in your pack as precautionary measures.

These preparations demonstrate respect for the environment and the personal journey you will experience.

You can always seek help because you don't have to understand everything independently. The visitor centers on both islands provide context and conversation along with place-based knowledge which cannot be duplicated by applications. Local staff members who work at visitor centers know which trails are washed out and which paths offer better sunrise views while also recommending those paths to walk another day.

If you're ever unsure, stop and ask. Visitors who show respect for their movement through the land earn appreciation from locals who are always ready to provide directions.

Hawaiian people give directions by smiling at you and sharing a story or advising you to proceed with care. The way directions here suggest you should move slowly.

Moving with Intention

Navigation represents more than moving between locations because it embodies your interaction with the world. Travel on Lanai and Molokai transcends mere transportation logistics. During your journey through Lanai and Molokai your movements create an interaction between yourself and the surrounding environment.

Here, the best paths aren't always paved. The clearest directions aren't always marked. The best memories generally happen outside of established time constraints. During a peaceful shuttle ride through taro fields you may discover clarity. The tranquility of a trail reveals its secrets when GPS signals disappear but your natural senses remain active.

Through these signs you learn reliance on natural landmarks—the coastline's curve and the trees' tilt with cultural words mauka and makai acting as a local compass. When you seek assistance you form bonds while unexpected routes reveal the true narrative hidden within.

This chapter focuses on more than just knowing how to travel from one place to another. It's about how to arrive—fully. Every motion you make on these islands, whether driving a 4x4 vehicle, taking an early-morning ferry ride or standing beside a quiet dirt road represents an opportunity to deepen your relationship with the location and its inhabitants as well as yourself.

No matter if your journey takes you through sunshine or rainstorms and across red land or salty air make sure to stay aware when traveling. Move with humility. The act of navigation here extends beyond holding an actual map. You must map your inner journey as you navigate these places.

Chapter Eight

Culinary Delights

H awaiian food is rooted in the idea of nourishment beyond the plate. Some dishes are simple, some complex, but all are grounded in the relationship between land, sea, and community. Two of the most enduring staples—poke and poi—carry that legacy in every bite.

Explore Iconic Hawaiian Dishes

The dish poke stands out as the first recognizable food to visitors. The dish consists of raw ahi tuna cubes and a mix of sea salt, seaweed, soy sauce, and sesame oil with optional chili or green onion.

Fishermen used poke as a quick snack to savor their daily catch without much effort. The islands now offer multiple different versions of this dish at both casual eateries and sophisticated dining establishments. Despite the evolution of its ingredients, the core principles of freshness, balance, and fish respect remain consistent in the dish.

Poi tells a quieter, deeper story. Native Hawaiian culture attributes deep spiritual and ancestral significance to the taro root used to make this dish. The taro root undergoes steam cooking and then manual pounding while water is gradually added to produce the characteristic smooth, thick paste. The paste maintains an earthy taste that develops a slight tanginess during the fermentation process. Poi maintains a subtle flavor profile while possessing significant cultural importance. The food serves to stabilize both the meal itself and the individuals who eat together.

Culinary History and Context

Within Hawaiian culture, kalo and taro represent something greater than agricultural produce. People view it as an ancestral figure that represents a direct link to the act of creation. Eating poi represents a tribute to ancestral ties and cultural heritage.

The cultural practice of eating poi from a communal bowl served to strengthen social bonds by emphasizing unity and community connections. The dish of poke demonstrates the flexible lifestyle of islanders who rely on ocean resources. The food derives from instinctual choices and available supplies based on the sea's offerings and the cultural respect it receives.

The preparation and consumption of both dishes represent core elements of Hawaiian daily routines and important ceremonial events. Sacred ceremonies and family celebrations commonly featured poi as a staple dish. When poi appeared on the dining surface, it represented ancestral connections rather than just sustenance.

Preparation and Tasting Tips

Poi takes time to grow on people because it has a unique texture and taste. People who are experiencing this dish for the first time may find its texture and taste unfamiliar. You should serve it as a complement to salty or savory dishes such as kalua pig or lomi salmon. Experience poi as a flavor complement rather than consuming it like a dip. Traditionally people eat it with their fingers to create a tactile connection to the eating experience. When selecting poke, prioritize fresh dishes and steer clear of excessive toppings. Let the fish lead.

When preparing either dish at home or sampling it for the first time, you should experience it at a leisurely pace. When dining on these meals, take your time to savor them through curious exploration.

Seek Out Local Recommendations

Locals know the best spots for poke, so ask them about their favorite places. A humble corner café on Lanai serves fresh fish caught that morning. Island families run shops and small markets on Molokai that sell traditional house-made products passed down through generations. Fresh poi proves difficult to locate since traditional preparation methods require significant time. Visit farmers markets alongside cultural centers and restaurants that feature locally sourced ingredients. The true essence of poi becomes apparent when you get to experience it at a community gathering or luau event.

Scenic Dining Locations

Dining on Lanai isn't about excess. The dining experience here combines delicious meals with serene surroundings to bring peace to the mind. Beachfront eateries and dining areas packed with tourists are nonexistent here. The island provides personal dining spaces nestled within landscapes that seem almost sacred.

The best dining experience is found at open-air restaurants above Hulopoe Bay that offer views of the ocean's changing hues. Your table offers views of spinner dolphins swimming offshore along with sun rays slipping behind distant cliffs. As dusk settles on a cloudless night, the heavens transform into an art display while the meal becomes a part of the performance.

Dining in Lanai City offers patrons an introspective experience through unique perspectives that focus inward instead of outward. Cafés and eateries sit within the embrace of pine-lined streets and plantation-style architecture, creating spaces that residents view more as community gathering points than traditional dining establishments. The simple setting turns into its own form of beauty when you sit on a shaded porch or by a window facing Dole Park.

Ambiance and Atmosphere

Lanai's dining establishments specialize in sophisticated tranquility as their ambiance. Tables maintain ample space between them while music remains at a soft volume when present. You can hear natural sounds like tree wind and distant ocean waves between the courses in this type of place. Even upscale restaurants here feel relaxed. The venue doesn't require formal attire but invites guests to show up in their personal style.

In town, meals often unfold slowly. Locals stop to chat. Servers remember your name. The gentle atmosphere reflects the island's nature because it embodies a slow-paced environment without noise where presence matters most.

Highlights and Recommendations

Dishes such as pan-seared opakapaka (pink snapper) and grilled mahi-mahi with citrus glaze dominate the menu as local seafood takes center stage. Local chefs establish close partnerships with farms around them to design menus that change according to seasonal growth. Island-raised meats together with sweet potatoes and tropical fruits join fresh greens as key ingredients in straightforward yet fresh dishes.

Consider enjoying a fresh salad made from upcountry greens or savoring a poke bowl alongside taro chips for a lighter meal option. When you're eating close to the shoreline, inquire about the morning's catch since it frequently appears on the dinner menu.

Insider Tips for Dining Reservations

The dining options on Lanai remain limited in number, with restricted seating availability at popular areas, including Hulopoe Bay. You need to secure your reservation at least one day ahead of time if you plan to enjoy dinner during sunset. It's advisable to confirm restaurant hours because some establishments modify their operating schedule with each season or reserve their space for private functions.

To enhance your dining experience, schedule your reservation shortly before the golden hour begins. Your journey begins in daylight as you observe the landscape transform into softer hues, which concludes with a meal under visible stars.

Unique Dining Opportunities

Molokai doesn't do flash. This culinary scene offers intimate dining experiences that connect communities through deeply traditional foodways. Multi-page menus and high-concept plating designs are not part of Molokai's dining experience. The flavors you encounter will evoke a sense of home cooking even when you're experiencing someone else's culinary heritage.

Authentic meals from the island exist at locations you might overlook if you didn't search for them. Family eateries, along with roadside food stalls and communal hall dinners, deliver meals that embody both heartfelt cooking and historical significance. The island's authentic culinary experience includes kalua pig, squid luau, and haupia because these dishes represent the actual meals people regularly consume. Here, casual dining involves receiving a foil-wrapped plate lunch as someone gives you a friendly nod and smile.

Community luaus act as an extensive showcase of Molokai's food traditions. These are more than meals—they're cultural expressions. Shared dishes and storytelling alongside music merge together to blur the distinction between guests and family members.

Farm-to-Table

The true essence of Molokai food comes not from the recipe but from where the ingredients originate. The majority of meal components reach diners after being produced or harvested from local farms and watersheds close to their final destination. Small farms cultivate taro, sweet potatoes, bananas, and papayas through traditional farming techniques that focus on sustainable practices and land respect.

Both chefs and home cooks frequently choose to utilize local ingredients instead of bringing in supplies from elsewhere. Fish is caught fresh. Vegetables are seasonal. The community directly provides neighbors with their supply of eggs and herbs as well as honey. This authentic farm-to-table practice exists independently of tourism marketing—it represents local lifestyle norms.

You'll taste that simplicity in every bite.

Each Sunday morning a local chef acquired her cooking skills by observing her grandmother make laulau, which involved wrapping pork and butterfish in taro leaves using her grandmother's memory-driven movements. A lunch counter operator keeps traditions alive by pounding poi manually to prepare family recipes that have been handed down through three generations before sunrise.

The food culture here relies heavily on these stories because they represent its foundational elements. Meals come with lineage. Flavor comes with family. If you engage in conversation with the food preparers, you will usually learn about the origins of their ingredients and the reasons behind their cooking methods.

These aren't performances—they're memories, shared openly.

Culinary Tours

Molokai provides small-scale culinary tours for visitors who want an immersive experience that extends beyond simple food tasting. Certain tours bring you to nearby farms so you can explore loʻi fields by foot while learning how taro is grown and making poi yourself with hand-pounding techniques. Some tours will instruct you on harvesting before leading a cooking class with your collected ingredients.

Local residents who possess extensive knowledge of their cultural traditions operate these tours, which emphasize respect together with educational and preservation goals above entertainment. Food consumption extends beyond mere eating because it helps us understand how it defines our identity.

Sustainability in Dining

Residents of Lanai and Molokai live sustainably as an essential part of their everyday existence. The concept of responsible dining takes on significant importance in areas with scarce resources and distant supply networks where cultural respect for the environment dominates. Your dining choices represent more than personal taste, as they help maintain the islands' ecosystems and economies, which protect cultural values that sustain their integrity.

The practice of sustainable dining in this region represents the indigenous Hawaiian concept of mālama 'āina, which means caring for the land. The restaurant's care is demonstrated in its ingredient sourcing methods and waste reduction efforts along with environmental stewardship practices inside and outside the kitchen.

Restaurants Leading the Way

Numerous restaurants on Lanai and Molokai demonstrate sustainable practices even though they don't actively promote them. Restaurants source their ingredients from local farms and nearby fishing operations because practicality and respect guide their food choices rather than following current trends. Several restaurants manage their kitchen waste by composting food scraps, while others eliminate single-use plastics or utilize solar power for kitchen operations.

Eateries on Molokai regularly update their menus based on seasonal ingredients available that day or week. Chefs on Lanai work together with local farms and fishermen to get ingredients straight from their source, which maintains freshness and helps their neighbors. These restaurants show their dedication to the land through their sustainable practices despite lacking official certifications.

Tips for Supporting Sustainable Practices

Travelers possess greater power to effect change than they generally realize. Begin your inquiry by questioning the origins of the food and its preparation methods as well as waste management techniques. Opt for establishments that openly disclose their practices and help smaller venues that demonstrate higher responsibility despite limited resources.

If you order takeout, bring your own reusable utensils and containers. Do not use disposable plastic bottles, and refrain from requesting a straw unless absolutely required. Take advantage of composting or recycling options when provided by a restaurant. The seemingly minor actions we take become significant contributions, particularly in areas where nature and human expansion maintain a fragile equilibrium.

Sustainability Initiatives

Should you feel motivated to deepen your impact here, you should think about joining local sustainability efforts. Local farms organize volunteer days for planting and harvesting crops. Some organizations conduct workshops that teach traditional cooking techniques alongside sustainable farming methods. Community garden projects and food sovereignty forums permit entry to visitors who show curiosity and respect.

You can make an impact without fundamentally changing your way of life. A powerful start involves showing up with an open mind and supporting businesses that care about their impact while asking thoughtful questions.

Sustainable dining on the islands represents an ongoing effort rather than achieving perfection. It's about attention. The process of honoring food involves recognizing the journey from soil through to plate and beyond, recognizing that our eating habits define our travel experiences and personal identity.

Eating With Intention

The food experiences on Lanai and Molokai deliver nourishment beyond physical sustenance. Taro leaves and tide-fresh fish become a cultural gateway that establishes a common language. Food transforms into a connection between tourists and locals as well as between history and present life when you eat poke while still on the beach or learn traditional poi preparation beside someone with ancestral knowledge.

The islands do not require you to search for the ideal bite. The islands ask you to trace the origins of each bite. Seek answers about who made the meal and the environmental elements that enabled its creation. When you eat at this location, you take part in the experience by consuming food through respectful curiosity.

When you experience local dishes or test new foods at community gatherings, take a moment. Taste slowly. Ask questions. Say thank you. The presentation of your food, whether it comes in banana leaves or white linen, carries meaning beyond its taste. It holds story, memory, and connection.

This type of nourishment lasts with you well after you've finished your meal.

Chapter Nine

Accommodation Insights

There's something quietly transformative about stepping into a space where every detail has been crafted not just for comfort, but for presence. On Lanai and Molokai, luxury doesn't shout. It whispers through thoughtful design, unobstructed views, and experiences that unfold at your pace. Here, exclusivity isn't about distance from others—it's about proximity to nature, wellness, and stillness.

Luxurious Escapes — Exclusive Resorts

Lanai's oceanfront luxury redefines the concept of a resort stay. Perched above a protected marine sanctuary, one of the island's most refined properties is built into the cliffs with an elegance that feels effortless. From the moment you arrive, there's a rhythm that takes hold—a softened tempo that begins with the hush of ocean breeze and carries through every space you inhabit.

Guest rooms and suites blend seamlessly with the environment, using natural textures and open-air layouts to create a sense of quiet immersion. Private lanais open onto sweeping views of the Pacific, while interior spaces feel both refined and grounded. Dining is a celebration of the island's bounty—fresh fish, local greens, and tropical fruits prepared with precision and care. The atmosphere encourages you to linger, to savor, and to reconnect.

Just inland, nestled among the misty upland pines, a separate wellness-focused resort offers a more introspective version of luxury. This is not a place for crowds or spectacle. It's a retreat built around intentional living, holistic health, and personalized growth. Whether you come for yoga at sunrise, private thermal garden soaks, or simply the chance to breathe without interruption, every moment is curated for restoration.

Here, staff take on the role of wellness guides—offering one-on-one support to help you design an experience around movement, nourishment, and stillness. Spa treatments draw from both Eastern and Hawaiian traditions, using local ingredients and centuries-old techniques. Meals are plant-forward, beautifully plated, and designed to fuel both body and clarity. You won't find excess here—only what serves your well-being.

Both resorts are positioned with care. The oceanside retreat offers direct access to the crescent-shaped beach at Hulopoe Bay, known for its crystal waters and vibrant reef. The wellness enclave, meanwhile, sits high enough in the hills to offer sweeping island views and a sense of quiet separation from the world below.

When it comes to booking, timing can elevate the experience even further. Visiting during quieter shoulder seasons often allows for greater privacy and easier access to signature experiences. Some travelers opt into loyalty programs or resort packages that bundle accommodations with guided excursions, spa treatments, or private tours. These options often strike a balance between indulgence and value.

On islands where nature is revered and silence is sacred, luxury means more than thread counts and cocktails by the pool. It's the kind of luxury that invites you to slow down. To listen more closely. To rest not just your body, but your attention.

This isn't just about where you stay. It's about how you feel while staying there—and long after you've left.

Budget-Friendly Lodging — Lanai's Hidden Gems

You don't need five stars to have a five-star experience. On Lanai, simplicity can be just as memorable as luxury—especially when it comes with local charm, warm hospitality, and the kind of quiet that money can't buy. For travelers who value authenticity over opulence, Lanai offers a small but meaningful range of accommodations that keep you close to the island's heart.

Tucked into the peaceful streets of Lanai City is a historic inn that's been welcoming visitors since the plantation era. With its plantation-style architecture, creaky floorboards, and wraparound porch, it feels more like a family home than a hotel. Rooms are cozy, thoughtfully restored, and intentionally unflashy. Mornings might begin with locally brewed coffee on the veranda and conversations with other travelers who, like you, came in search of something different—something quieter.

This kind of stay comes with a certain rhythm. You might stroll to a local café for breakfast, then walk a few blocks to find art galleries or small shops run by longtime residents. There's no valet here, no on-demand concierge—but there's a kind of hospitality that feels more personal, more human.

Not far from the town square, another option offers a more communal and adventurous vibe. Popular with solo travelers and backpackers, this budget-friendly hostel provides shared dorms and private rooms at prices that leave room in your travel budget for experiences. While modest in its offerings, it delivers where it counts—clean spaces, a friendly atmosphere, and the kind of casual community where stories are swapped over shared meals or island maps are spread out on common room tables.

Choosing locally owned lodging not only makes economic sense—it makes ethical sense. Your stay supports real people, not chains. You help sustain businesses that have been part of the island's story for decades. And more often than not, your hosts will offer insights no guidebook ever could—directions to an unmarked trail, tips on where to catch the sunset without a crowd, or the name of someone who leads a tour you won't find online.

Booking these hidden gems usually requires a bit more research. They may not always show up at the top of popular travel sites, and availability can be limited—especially during local festivals or holiday weeks. But for those willing to dig a little deeper and book a little earlier, the rewards are real.

Many past guests describe these stays not just as places to sleep but as the backdrop for some of their favorite memories. It's in these smaller lodgings that you're more likely to be greeted by name, handed a fresh guava from the garden, or invited to a neighborhood gathering. These aren't amenities you can advertise—but they're the ones you'll remember.

On Lanai, less can truly be more. And in these quiet, character-filled lodgings, you'll find that what your trip lacks in opulence, it more than makes up for in meaning.

Molokai's Boutique Inns

Molokai doesn't cater to the masses. It doesn't chase trends or strive to impress with polish. Instead, it offers travelers something far more enduring: places to stay that feel deeply connected to the land, the culture, and the community. Boutique inns on Molokai are not just about accommodations—they're about storytelling.

One of the island's most beloved inns sits just outside the main town of Kaunakakai, nestled between palms and sea spray. The buildings are modest, with their roots in the mid-20th century, but the experience they offer is far richer than their exterior suggests. Rooms open directly onto the shoreline, with the ocean close enough that you can hear the tide rolling in before you see it. Step outside, and you're likely to find a fisherman casting a net, a child gathering driftwood, or a neighbor walking barefoot with their morning coffee.

What makes stays like these so distinct is their sense of place. Décor isn't curated to be trendy—it reflects history. You'll find furniture built by local hands, artwork that tells ancestral stories, and architectural details that nod to the island's plantation past. These aren't design choices—they're memories made visible.

Some of these inns are housed in restored buildings with histories stretching back generations. Others were built by families who still live on the island and manage the properties themselves. The result is a hospitality style that feels less like service and more like stewardship. You're not just a guest—you're a visitor being welcomed into a space that carries meaning.

There's also a surprising richness in the small details. Breakfast may come with papaya picked from a tree outside the kitchen window. A bookshelf in the lounge might hold donated paperbacks alongside local folklore. A staff member might remember your name not from a reservation system, but because they chatted with you at the farmers market earlier that day.

Because many of these inns are small—some with fewer than a dozen rooms—booking in advance is recommended, especially during cultural festivals or holiday weekends. Direct booking is often the best way to secure a reservation and opens the door to personalized communication before you even arrive. It also allows you to support the innkeepers directly.

While you won't find valet parking or 24-hour room service, you will find something far rarer: the chance to stay in a place that reflects the island's values. Simplicity. Humility. Connection.

Molokai's boutique inns may be tucked away in quiet corners, but for those who stay, they become the backdrop to some of the most meaningful parts of the journey—sunrises watched alone, conversations shared with strangers-turned-friends, and the slow realization that comfort isn't always measured in amenities.

Sometimes, it's measured in feeling at home in a place that isn't yours—and knowing you're welcome anyway.

Sustainable Accommodation Choices

The choice of accommodation matters as much as your approach to exploration in Hawaii because the delicate balance between human life and natural life makes it so. Guests at sustainable accommodations in Lanai and Molokai can rest assured their stay honors local communities while protecting the land and reducing their impact without losing comfort.

Residents of both islands understand that genuine hospitality means welcoming visitors while also protecting their natural environment. Eco-conscious resorts operating with solar power and small lodges that recycle rainwater represent this philosophy, while guesthouses demonstrate thoughtful living through locally sourced breakfasts and biodegradable bath products.

Properties across various regions now consider renewable energy essential rather than a gimmick.

Many off-grid accommodations in remote areas of Molokai use solar-powered systems to provide lighting and heat water. Architectural designs frequently incorporate passive cooling elements such as large windows that harness trade winds and layouts that utilize natural elements for comfort while relying on fans instead of air conditioning.

Materials matter, too. The trend for eco-friendly building materials now shows bamboo flooring alongside recycled furnishings and non-toxic paints surpassing synthetic choices. In place of plastic or imported ornaments, environmental respect is shown through décor choices that incorporate driftwood, local flora, and handmade items.

The hospitality at these places stands out because it truly stands out. The employees working in these facilities belong to the communities they support. During their free time, many staff members work as cultural educators, farmers, or conservation volunteers. Guests have opportunities to participate in community initiatives, which include beach cleanups as well as native plant restoration projects and wetland educational walks.

Travelers who want to find sustainable lodging options can rely on several useful indicators. Traveler reviews from environmentally conscious guests provide beneficial insights alongside certifications such as Green Key or LEED.

Analyzing how a property discusses sustainability will reveal their commitment to environmentally friendly practices. Do these efforts form an integral part of guest experiences or appear solely as marketing elements? The difference matters.

Choosing sustainable accommodations requires more than simply selecting places that offer green towel options. Investing in this form of tourism generates greater benefits than its consumption. Every overnight stay makes an environmental impact, so you should aim to minimize your footprint.

Several properties encourage visitors to take part in their conservation activities at the site. Properties allow guests to participate in vegetable harvesting for communal meals, native tree planting initiatives, or educational sessions about land management with local experts. These activities serve as invitations for guests to learn how to appreciate and understand the land through its own unique characteristics.

Selecting eco-friendly accommodation demonstrates respect. For the earth. For the culture. For the generations who will come after. Travelers who choose sustainable stays on Lanai or Molokai become part of the islands' deep-rooted relationship between people and place because their choices leave a lasting memory.

Where You Stay Is How You Travel

The sleeping area functions as a base camp where travelers rest before facing new adventures each day. On Lanai and Molokai, places of stay become more than just overnight stays. It becomes part of the story.

The setting of your room along the island determines whether you're wrapped in the silence of a cliffside suite or sitting on the lanai of a beachfront cottage with the ocean nearby. Choosing where to stay in this place goes beyond practical needs because it also touches your personal side.

Luxury doesn't always mean extravagance. Sometimes it's wellness woven into every detail. The luxury manifests through handwritten messages on your pillow or garden views that defy photographic capture. Staying at a boutique inn allows visitors to understand Molokai's spirit better than reading any guidebook can. Staying on a budget in Lanai City could result in making new friends and conversations that reshape your perspective of the island.

Choosing to stay in a manner that respects the land through sustainable practices transforms you into more than just a traveler. Your role transitions into shared responsibility as you actively contribute to protecting the islands' unique aspects.

The way you choose to stay on Lanai and Molokai reflects more than just luxury or simpler living. They're about alignment. With nature. With culture. The tranquil aspects of our being that get overshadowed in noisier environments.

Where you stay is how you travel. Every stay here presents travelers with opportunities to prioritize meaningful experiences over superficial ones and to follow deliberate choices rather than spontaneous actions.

Chapter Ten

Local Culture and Traditions

Malama Aina—The Practice of Caring for the Land

In Hawaiian, *malama* means "to care for," and *'āina* means "land." But like most things in Hawaiian culture, the meaning of *malama 'āina* runs far deeper than translation. It's not simply a practice—it's a worldview, a responsibility, and a way of living in relationship with place. To *malama 'āina* is to care for the land as a family member, not a resource. The land is not owned; it is honored.

This mindset is woven into stories, ceremonies, and daily life across the islands. It reflects the understanding that everything in nature is interconnected: the mountains feed the rain, the rain nourishes the taro, and the taro feeds the people. And in return, people are expected to care for the mountains. This cycle is not romanticized nostalgia—it's ecological truth wrapped in cultural wisdom.

For visitors, understanding this concept is essential. Not because it's a quaint idea to admire, but because it's alive. And it invites participation.

Ancient Roots, Living Practice

Long before Western systems of land ownership and extraction took hold, Native Hawaiians practiced a sophisticated land management system based on *malama 'āina*. One of the most powerful examples is the *ahupua'a* system—a division of land that ran from mountain to sea. Each *ahupua'a* included the full range of ecological zones needed for sustainable living: upland forests for timber and birds, fertile valleys for agriculture, and nearshore reefs for fishing.

People cared for their section of the land with a deep sense of kuleana—responsibility. Resources were shared, not hoarded. Seasons were observed. Ceremonies marked planting and harvest cycles. And if the land suffered, the people knew it was a reflection of imbalance.

This system wasn't just efficient. It was spiritual. The land was considered sacred. And though centuries of colonization disrupted that system, the values behind it endure.

Community Stewardship Today

Across Lanai and Molokai, the practice of *malama 'āina* continues—not just in principle, but in action. On Molokai especially, the connection between people and place remains tightly held. Community groups organize regular beach cleanups, native plant restorations, and taro patch revivals, often with the help of students, elders, and families working side by side.

At Halawa Valley on Molokai's east end, for example, families have returned to restore *lo'i kalo*—traditional taro patches—that had gone dormant for decades. Visitors who join the effort quickly find that the work is not just about clearing brush or digging ditches. It's about learning to observe, listen, and move in rhythm with the land. The elders don't shout instructions—they teach by doing, by storytelling, and by quiet example.

On Lanai, conservationists and volunteers collaborate on habitat protection and reforestation efforts. Guided hikes into the uplands often include time spent planting native trees or removing invasive species. These efforts don't seek to freeze the land in time but to help it recover its balance.

Traditional Methods, Modern Tools

While the roots of *malama 'āina* are ancient, the tools used today are often modern. Drones monitor erosion. GPS mapping helps track native plant restoration. Solar-powered water pumps irrigate *lo'i*. But the spirit behind the work remains the same: observe the land, respond with care, and think in terms of generations—not profits or convenience.

One notable example is the use of traditional fishponds, or *loko i'a*, especially on Molokai. These engineered coastal structures—some built hundreds of years ago—are being restored with the help of ecologists and community leaders. They're not just functional; they're part of a larger story about food sovereignty and ecological intelligence.

How Visitors Can Participate

Visitors often ask, "What can I do that actually helps?" The answer is simple: show up with humility. Respect comes before involvement.

Many community organizations across the islands welcome respectful participation in conservation activities. These might include taro patch workdays, reef cleanups, or native plant nurseries open to volunteers. These aren't photo ops—they're opportunities to contribute. To give back to a place that's already given you beauty, silence, and awe.

If you're not able to volunteer physically, you can still support the work. Choose eco-conscious tour operators. Stay in accommodations that partner with conservation efforts. Donate to local land trusts or cultural education nonprofits. And perhaps most importantly—practice awareness. Stay on marked trails. Don't touch coral. Don't take rocks or shells. Speak softly in wild places.

The Deeper Takeaway

Caring for the land isn't a tourist activity—it's a way of thinking that extends long after your flight home. It reshapes how you see your own backyard. How you eat. How you move through spaces that aren't yours.

When you hike through a reforested ridge or kneel in the muddy water of a taro patch, you begin to understand something: the land remembers how it's treated. And those who listen—really listen—are changed by what they hear.

The Art of Lei Making—A Symbol of Aloha

To someone unfamiliar with Hawaiian culture, a lei might appear to be just a beautiful necklace made of flowers. But in truth, a lei is never just decorative. It's an offering. A gesture. A story told in petals, leaves, and sometimes even shells, seeds, or feathers. In Hawaii, leis are woven with meaning and intention, and giving one is an act of aloha—expressing love, welcome, gratitude, or remembrance.

You'll see leis at graduations, birthdays, weddings, and memorials. But they're not reserved only for milestones. In Hawaiian culture, a lei might be given just because. To show respect. To honor a moment. To let someone know they matter. When a lei is placed around your shoulders, it's not simply a gift—it's a connection.

Traditional Techniques and Materials

Lei making is a practice that dates back centuries, passed from generation to generation not through textbooks, but through hands. Each island, each family, and sometimes each individual lei maker has their own style and approach. But there are foundational techniques that root the tradition.

Some leis are woven using the *wili* method—twisting materials around a central cord. Others are braided (*haku*) or strung like beads (*kui*). The choice of method often depends on the materials used, the purpose of the lei, and the personality of the maker.

Materials are gathered with care, often from the mountains or garden. Plumeria, lehua blossoms, maile vines, ti leaves, and palapalai ferns are among the most cherished. Each carries symbolic weight. Maile, for instance, is used in ceremonies and represents honor and peace. Lehua is linked to Pele, the goddess of volcanoes. Even the act of gathering plants—known as *laʻau picking*—is considered sacred, done with prayer and permission.

Time slows during lei making. It has to. The process asks for attention, presence, and care. In this way, the act of creation becomes just as important as the final piece.

Modern Adaptations and Innovations

Like all living traditions, lei making has evolved. Today, you'll find leis made with everything from orchids and roses to yarn, candy, ribbon, and even dollar bills. While some of these variations are created for novelty or convenience, others represent creative expressions of aloha adapted for contemporary life.

Many lei makers today blend old and new materials, incorporating non-native flowers alongside traditional greenery or designing pieces with bold, sculptural flair. These modern leis often reflect personal style, regional influence, or the event they're meant to celebrate. Some are designed to be worn only briefly; others are dried and preserved as keepsakes.

Importantly, even as styles shift, the core remains the same: each lei is made with intention. It still holds meaning. It still asks to be treated with respect.

Learning the Craft

If you want to learn lei making, the best way is to sit with someone who practices it. On both Lanai and Molokai, local cultural centers and artisans offer lei-making workshops that are open to visitors. These classes don't just teach technique—they offer a deeper understanding of the cultural values behind the practice.

You'll learn how to identify local plants, prepare them properly, and weave them with care. More than that, you'll be taught when and how to give a lei, how to receive one graciously, and how to treat it after it's worn. In Hawaiian tradition, leis are never thrown in the trash. They're returned to nature—buried, burned, or placed in a meaningful spot—so that the love and mana within them continues to circulate.

Even if you're not the one doing the weaving, just witnessing the process can deepen your appreciation. The act itself is a form of quiet ceremony. And when you give or receive a lei with this understanding, it becomes something more than a souvenir. It becomes a thread in a larger cultural tapestry—one you've been gently welcomed into.

Local Music and Dance—A Cultural Exploration

In Hawaii, music and dance aren't just entertainment. They're memories in motion. They're how stories are passed on, how emotions are honored, and how history is kept alive. To experience traditional Hawaiian music and dance is to witness culture speaking in its native tongue—not through facts, but through feeling.

At the heart of this expression is **hula**. Contrary to popular images of grass skirts and ukuleles, hula is a deeply spiritual and disciplined art form. It's a dance of purpose, used to honor ancestors, mark sacred events, or share genealogies and legends. Every movement of the hand, every sway of the hips, and every step is intentional. Hula is not improvised. It's choreographed storytelling—each gesture rooted in meaning.

Hula is often accompanied by **oli**—chants that carry the weight of history. These chants don't rhyme or follow predictable melodies. They rise and fall like wind through the trees, delivered in tones that recall the cadence of the land itself. Oli can be prayers, proclamations, or ceremonial welcomes. They were once used in place of written language to record knowledge, and today, they remain an essential part of ceremonies, gatherings, and teaching.

Traditional Instruments and Sound

The soundtrack of Hawaii extends far beyond the strum of a ukulele. Traditional instruments include the *pahu* (a carved wooden drum covered in sharkskin), *ipu* (gourd percussion), and *pu* (conch shell). These tools create rhythms that are primal, grounding, and unmistakably Hawaiian.

Each instrument has a role. The *pahu*, for example, was once reserved for sacred hula and religious ceremonies. Its steady, thunderous beat signals formality, gravitas, and ancestral presence. In contrast, the *ukulele*, which was introduced to Hawaii in the 19th century by Portuguese immigrants, brought a lighter, melodic tone that blended beautifully into the islands' evolving soundscape.

Today, many musicians blend traditional instruments with guitar, slack key, and even jazz or reggae influences, creating modern Hawaiian music that is both rooted and fresh. This evolution reflects a living culture—not frozen in time, but responsive and resilient.

Styles Old and New

Hula itself comes in two primary forms: *hula kahiko*, the ancient style, and *hula 'auana*, the modern adaptation. *Kahiko* is performed to chants and traditional percussion and often tells sacred stories. The movements are strong, purposeful, and grounded. *'Auana*, on the other hand, is more fluid and melodic, usually danced to contemporary Hawaiian music. It reflects the openness and influence of more recent generations.

Both styles are valued. Both are practiced. And both are taught with the same reverence for lineage and discipline. It's not uncommon for a dancer to train for years before performing in public. The expectation isn't perfection—it's presence.

Where to Experience It

On both Lanai and Molokai, opportunities to witness live music and dance happen in community spaces more often than on formal stages. You might hear a group of aunties singing in harmony at a weekend market or see keiki (children) performing hula at a local festival. Cultural centers, community centers, and small resorts often host performances that are free and open to the public.

Molokai's *Ka Hula Piko* festival, for example, celebrates the origins of hula and brings together dancers, chanters, and practitioners from across the islands. On Lanai, smaller gatherings and storytelling nights often incorporate music, giving visitors a chance to experience performance in a setting that feels personal, not packaged.

Participating with Respect

If you feel inspired to try hula or learn an instrument while visiting, there are ways to do so respectfully. Many local instructors offer beginner-friendly workshops, especially through cultural learning centers or educational programs. These classes often start not with dance moves or strumming techniques, but with context—language, story, and protocol.

Participation is welcomed but always approached with humility. You're not learning to perform—you're learning to understand. That mindset makes all the difference.

Whether you sit quietly in the back row of a chant circle or try your first basic hula step under the guidance of a local teacher, the experience stays with you. Music and dance in Hawaii are not performances for applause. They are offerings. And when you take part, you're not just a spectator—you become part of the story.

Understanding Kapu and Respecting Sacred Sites

A kapu system consisting of sacred rules and taboos directed every facet of life in traditional Hawaiian culture. Although the word translates as both "forbidden" and "sacred," its meaning extends beyond just being a restriction. The kapu system served as a moral, spiritual, and social structure that directed human behavior while safeguarding natural resources and maintaining harmony among people, land, and deities.

The regulations specified rules for fishing seasons and gender roles alongside guidelines for food preparation and sharing. Breaking kapu rules had spiritual consequences because it disrupted the community's divine balance. The outcomes reached extreme levels of severity and resulted in death in some cases.

The kapu system was officially ended in the early 19th century, but its influence continues. The concept of kapu influences modern speech regarding sacred sites and customary practices. Signs placed near heiau (temples) display the word kapu to inform visitors that entry is prohibited. Elders recount the stories about locations where powerful events took place because they remain present in their narratives. The deep cultural respect Hawaiians maintain for their land and spiritual spaces continues to be shaped by traditional values.

Sacred Sites and Their Significance

The landscape of Lanai and Molokai contains historical connections beyond its visual appeal. Scattered across the islands are places where the past feels particularly close: ancient fishponds stand alongside natural landscape formations and ceremonial sites with stone temples throughout the islands.

Stone platforms used for offerings and prayer stand out as the most visible historic Hawaiian structures. Every platform had a distinct function, which included agricultural use, military application, navigational guidance, or healing services. These were not places of casual visitation. These locations functioned as spiritual hubs where profound ceremonies took place and where visitors approached with deep reverence.

In addition to constructed landmarks, there exist natural places that people regard as sacred. Ancient tales of gods and battles, along with stories of love and transformations, have been preserved across generations in caves, cliffs, tidepools, and groves. You don't need to understand every detail of its history to appreciate the silent power emanating from that sacred space.

The island of Molokai contains multiple sacred spots that function as respected burial locations and oral history landmarks. The former exile site of Kalaupapa functions as a national historical park yet maintains personal significance for numerous families. When you visit these places, you should approach them with humility rather than just curiosity.

Guidelines for Visiting with Respect

When you encounter a kapu sign, ensure you respect its boundaries. It's not there for show. This sign asks for space while reminding visitors that certain locations should not be shared or photographed.

Exercise caution and respect while exploring public sacred sites. Stay on marked paths. Don't move or touch stones. Avoid loud conversations and eating or leaving offerings at sacred sites unless you receive an invitation to participate in a ceremony with such activities. Seek guidance from a local guide or cultural educator when you need clarification about protocol. People generally enjoy explaining the reasons behind the dos and don'ts when asked.

Photography is another area that requires sensitivity. Before snapping photos of sacred sites, you should seek permission and evaluate if experiencing the moment firsthand is more meaningful than documenting it. Recording certain places diminishes their power, as they derive strength from their privacy.

Deepening Understanding Through Education

Individuals seeking deeper knowledge about kapu and sacred sites have numerous options to expand their understanding. Native Hawaiian scholars' books and documentaries from community organizations, along with community elder-led tours, provide profound understanding that surpasses what can be learned from plaques or signs.

Organizations provide volunteer or educational programs that let people restore and care for sacred spaces so they can contribute beyond just visiting.

The most important lesson, though, may be this: reverence is not about knowing everything. It's about listening. Being present. You need to recognize that you are walking through someone else's story while showing respect.

Culture That Lives, Not Just Lasts

The traditional culture of Lanai and Molokai exists beyond what you can see at a glance. The culture of Lanai and Molokai exists beyond mere presentation and remains pure and authentic. It breathes. It shifts. The culture demands quiet recognition while seeking profound respect.

The activities you participate in during your visit to Lanai and Molokai represent more than traditional practices because they embody cultural continuity. These traditions and places continue to exist beyond the realm of historical artifacts. They are alive. Communities dedicated to these traditions act as living vessels that preserve and sustain their cultural heritage beyond mere memory.

Understanding that is where real appreciation begins. The purpose of your visit isn't to absorb every piece of information at once. It's about choosing to be present. To ask instead of assume. To walk slowly. To watch with care.

Modern travel activities mainly revolve around the capturing of moments. Hawaii's profound cultural encounters often go beyond what photos can capture. They'll live in the pauses. In the quiet nods. Your transformed view of the world becomes a permanent part of you after you return home.

The culture in this place exists independently of your need to take it in. The culture requires you to carry it with care.

Chapter Eleven

Hidden Gems and Offbeat Experiences

The farther you get from the map's bolded labels, the more Lanai begins to whisper. Its secrets aren't hidden exactly—they're just quiet. Especially along the island's northern coast, where sand meets wind and silence stretches wider than the horizon. Here, solitude isn't rare. It's expected. And for those willing to venture off the well-trodden routes, the beaches waiting at the edge of the island feel less like destinations and more like discoveries.

Kaiolohia Beach: Wreckage and Wonder

Known informally as Shipwreck Beach, Kaiolohia feels like something out of a storybook—remote, windblown, and marked by history. A rusted World War II-era tanker rests offshore, stranded in shallow waters where strong currents have thwarted vessels for centuries. It's not uncommon for visitors to stand on the sand, gazing out at the massive wreck, and feel something timeless stirring beneath the surface of the waves.

Getting here requires preparation. The beach lies near the northern tip of Lanai, reachable via an unpaved road best navigated with a high-clearance vehicle. Even then, the final approach often requires a short walk across uneven terrain. There's no signage to guide you—just instinct, direction, and the growing hush that marks your arrival.

The beach itself is not for swimming. The currents are unpredictable and strong. But the reward is visual and visceral: sculpted driftwood, raw coastline, and a landscape shaped more by wind than by human hands. Footprints are rare here. And silence, profound.

Polihua Beach: Where the Island Feels Endless

If Kaiolohia feels mysterious, Polihua Beach feels expansive. This stretch of golden sand runs for nearly two miles along Lanai's northwestern coast, facing out toward Molokai and the open Pacific. The beach is often completely empty, especially on weekdays. On still days, you might hear only the wind through ironwood trees and the rhythmic pull of waves across sand.

The journey to Polihua is not simple—but that's part of what keeps it pristine. Reaching the beach means taking an unpaved road that snakes through the Garden of the Gods. Along the way, the red earth gives way to shifting sand and coastal vegetation. Four-wheel-drive is essential, and conditions can change quickly after rainfall. Visitors should check weather forecasts and road conditions in advance.

Those who make it are rewarded not just with beauty, but with the sense of standing on the edge of something vast. In nesting season, you might spot green sea turtles resting on the shore. In the distance, the faint outline of Molokai rises like a dream. Time seems to stretch here—until it disappears altogether.

Finding the Hidden

Exploring Lanai's secret beaches requires a different kind of planning. These aren't places you stumble into. They ask for intention.

If you're heading out to Kaiolohia or Polihua, bring everything you'll need—water, snacks, sun protection, and a physical or downloaded map. Don't rely on cell signal to guide you. Let observation replace navigation. Notice the shifts in vegetation. The feel of the wind. The changing light.

Footwear should be sturdy. Sunscreen should be reef-safe. And time should be allowed to stretch—these aren't beaches to rush through.

Respecting What Remains Untouched

With solitude comes responsibility. These beaches remain untouched not by accident, but because of respect—by locals who avoid overexposing them, by travelers who leave nothing behind, and by the land itself, which makes no accommodations for thoughtless visitors.

Leave No Trace principles aren't just a courtesy here. They're a necessity. Pack out everything you bring in. Stay off dunes and vegetation. If you see marine life, observe quietly and from a distance.

On Polihua, where sea turtles sometimes nest, keep well clear of marked zones. At Kaiolohia, resist the temptation to climb or approach the wreck—it's unsafe, and its haunting presence is best honored from the shore.

The Beauty of Being Alone

There's a rare kind of peace in finding yourself on a beach where you're the only person for miles. The kind of peace that isn't performative or curated. The kind that just is.

Lanai doesn't flaunt these places. It offers them. Quietly. And if you come with care and curiosity, they'll reveal themselves to you—not all at once, but slowly. Like a tide pulling back to show what it's hidden beneath the surface.

Here, beauty isn't about what you capture. It's about what you witness—and who you become in the silence.

A Taste of Everyday Life

On Molokai, community doesn't just happen in homes or gathering halls—it happens in the open air, beneath tents and tarps, where the scent of ripe papaya mingles with ocean breeze and conversation carries across folding tables stacked with handmade goods. These are not tourist attractions. They're working markets, run by farmers, artists, aunties, and uncles. And if you want to feel the pulse of Molokai's everyday life, there's no better place to stand than beside a vendor sharing their crop or craft with open hands.

The Rhythm of the Market

The main farmers market in Kaunakakai unfolds slowly on weekend mornings. Locals arrive early, some with reusable bags slung over shoulders, others with keiki in tow. You'll see trucks pull up and transform into produce stalls within minutes. Bananas still attached to their stalks. Fresh-cut greens in plastic bins. Baskets of lilikoi, mango, and taro—often harvested just the day before.

Alongside the farmers are makers: soap crafters using coconut oil and island herbs, weavers offering lauhala bracelets, and elders selling jars of homemade jam from family recipes. These aren't just wares. They're pieces of lives lived in tune with the land.

There are no loudspeakers. No gimmicks. Just the hum of conversation, the clink of small bills changing hands, and the soft thump of shoes on dusty ground.

Pop-up markets happen across the island, often tied to community events or seasonal gatherings. You might stumble upon one near a beach park or after a local celebration. They appear as organically as the crops themselves—rooted in rhythm, not retail.

More Than a Transaction

To shop at a Molokai market is to engage—not just economically, but personally. It's common to hear stories behind what's on the table. A vendor might tell you how the rain shifted the flavor of this week's dragon fruit. Another might explain how their grandmother taught them to make lomi salmon, using the same sea salt they now sell by the pouch.

Questions are welcomed. Appreciation is encouraged. And while prices are fair, the real currency is connection. Ask someone where they grow their produce, and you may end up with directions to their farm. Compliment a quilt, and you could learn how the pattern honors a local legend.

These markets are places where heritage is folded into everyday items—and where buying local doesn't just support a person, it preserves a way of life.

Meeting the Makers

If you're looking for souvenirs that carry meaning, this is where you'll find them. Not mass-produced trinkets or airport-shop novelties, but handmade objects rooted in tradition and purpose.

Look for woven items crafted from hala leaves, jewelry made from shells and kukui nuts, and quilts that tell visual stories through color and stitch. Some artisans create natural dyes from native plants. Others work in reclaimed wood or volcanic stone. Every object holds a piece of the island's spirit—and often, the maker's hands were the only ones that touched it.

Tips for Meaningful Interactions

Go early: Produce is freshest at opening, and artisans often bring limited quantities.

Bring cash: While some vendors may accept digital payment, most rely on small bills.

Ask about the process: Makers love to share how things are grown, made, or designed—it's part of the experience.

Buy with intention: Even small purchases have big impact. Supporting a family-run farm or craft studio sustains more than a business—it helps protect a cultural thread.

What to Bring Home

Not everything you find can be taken home in a suitcase—but some things can.

Packable favorites include:

- Local honey and preserves

- Dried fruit and sea salt blends

- Handcrafted soaps and lotions made from native ingredients

- Small textiles, like hand-sewn pouches or placemats

- Simple jewelry with natural materials

Even if you don't buy anything, you'll likely carry something home with you anyway—a memory, a conversation, a moment where you felt welcomed not as a consumer, but as a guest.

The Market as a Mirror

Molokai's markets don't try to impress. They're not curated for outsiders. Their simple nature creates their true richness. They reflect the island's values: The island expresses its principles through markets that prioritize community needs above commercial interests while valuing slow sustainable practices as opposed to quick outcomes and preferring authentic narratives to flashy displays.

You'll discover more than what's in season after spending just one morning at this marketplace. The island maintains its unity by creating shared spaces and collective work and care instead of relying on signs or slogans.

As you depart your basket may contain numerous items. The emotional experience you acquire will remain with you longer than any physical items you take home.

Guided Tours with a Twist — Unique Perspectives

Not all tours are created equal. Some take you past places. Others take you into them.

The superior tours on Lanai and Molokai feature local guides rather than large vehicles or elaborate brochures. Residents of Lanai and Molokai lead these tours. The guides who lead the best tours have local knowledge about the trees' stories and the winds' strength along with unrecorded history. These unique tours transform you through their immersive experiences.

Walking Through Story

Cultural walking tours in both islands provide visitors with a slower yet more profound way to connect with the surroundings. While you may walk along coastal paths or ridge-top trails you are actually stepping through time. The guides combine local folklore with historical facts to explain both what visitors observe and its significance.

A guided tour across Keahiakawelo's red earth on Lanai reveals ancient priest battles and spiritual sites along with the stories behind the boulder-filled terrain. Sacred locations around Halawa Valley in Molokai form the basis of cultural excursions which delve into historical chants and tales of early settlers while teaching about how the environment continues to influence its people.

These experiences aren't just informative. They're immersive. Your experience will deepen your understanding of place and develop a more respectful and curious way of navigating through it.

The Rise of Eco-Tours

There's a quiet shift happening across the islands: a move toward conservation-centered tourism. These aren't tours built around spectacle. They're built around stewardship.

Eco-guides conduct hikes that function as educational experiences. You will gain knowledge about endemic species as well as reforestation initiatives while learning about traditional agricultural methods. A guide will demonstrate the restoration process of native plants to combat erosion. A guide demonstrates how ancient Hawaiian aquaculture techniques continue to shape today's food sustainability efforts.

Participants get to engage in activities during these tours rather than merely observing them. During the tour you might receive an invitation to plant seedlings or monitor tidepools while working to remove invasive species from the hillside. When you participate in these activities you make the transition from visitor to caretaker even if it's only for a single afternoon.

Interactive Journeys

These tours provide cultural engagement through direct interaction with the island environment which serves as a living classroom.

Someone who comes from a family deeply rooted in lei-making tradition will lead you through a workshop in a shaded clearing. Participants can sit at wooden benches to learn the technique of stamping kapa cloth by applying natural dyes derived from island plants. These adventures stand as opportunities for participation and creation that build connections.

Nature walks can also include unexpected depth. During a forest trail walk your guide will stop to explain the plant's healing applications instead of teaching its name. Starting with birdwatching your hike may conclude with learning about celestial navigation.

The goal isn't performance—it's exchange. People leave these experiences with both knowledge and additional insight. You carry understanding.

The Value of Local Expertise

Island guides provide more than logistical help. The guides from these islands share their first-hand experiences and ancestral knowledge along with their personal connection to the land which becomes difficult to imitate.

They recognize when muddy conditions make the trail unsafe for hiking. They have determined which reef section becomes safe once the tide changes. Their personal connection to the place allows them to explain its significance without any scripted preparation.

When you hire local guides you ensure your travel spending benefits the community. The program assists families financially while maintaining cultural traditions and keeps storytelling with its rightful owners.

To locate these tours you can seek information at farmers markets or visitor centers and even ask your host. The finest guides typically don't rely on broad advertising instead people discover them through personal recommendations.

Something for Everyone

Photographers seeking golden light on cliff edges and food enthusiasts wanting to explore Molokai's agricultural history will find tours suitable for their interests. It is essential to search beyond what is immediately visible.

Photography tours provide access to hidden vantage points where you can observe light play across lava rock formations and forest canopies. Taro fields and aquaponic farms will become familiar sights as cooks demonstrate traditional dishes passed down through generations during food-focused tours.

Certain tours provide personal attention by allowing only two or three guests to explore with a guide. These community-based tours develop as group experiences which resemble social gatherings instead of conventional excursions.

Select a tour option that aligns with your speed of travel and personal interests while meeting your objectives. The most excellent experiences make room for silence while allowing questions to arise and welcome unexpected moments.

Nighttime Adventures — Stargazing and More

As the sun descends over Lanai and Molokai the landscape transforms into a serene beauty that moves at nature's pace under starlight instead of artificial lights. On these islands, night isn't an ending, it's the beginning. Stars illuminate the sky as sound fades and vision becomes sharper during this quiet time when the heavens reveal their tales.

The nighttime activities found on these islands differ greatly from those in urban areas. These islands lack busy nightclubs and illuminated city lines. Instead, there's stillness. There's sky. These islands offer a basic excitement because most people around the world are asleep as you experience them.

Stargazing Under Pristine Skies

The islands of Lanai and Molokai provide some of the clearest unpolluted skies found anywhere on Earth. Both islands maintain ideal conditions for stargazing because development levels remain low and artificial lighting outside town centers is negligible.

As you leave the coastal areas and ascend to higher elevations the sky appears larger and more expansive. The best spot to view stars on Lanai is just above Keahiakawelo where high altitude meets dry skies to display a full panorama of constellations. Breathtaking views await on Molokai at the east end near Halawa Valley or inland beyond the small towns along Kamehameha V Highway.

Stargazing tours led by astronomers and cultural practitioners who combine modern scientific knowledge with Hawaiian star stories operate in several specific locations. Polynesian navigators used celestial bodies such as the star Arcturus, known as Hōkūleʻa, to traverse thousands of miles across open oceans before modern navigation tools like GPS or compasses existed. Participants use telescopes and star charts and have the opportunity to relax and observe the night sky during these sessions.

All you require for personal stargazing includes just a blanket and a flashlight equipped with a red lens to preserve your night vision along with your sense of wonder. Allow your eyes several minutes to acclimate. Then look up. The experience of viewing the night sky can alter your perceptions of time and distance alongside your personal connection to the universe.

Moonlit Hikes and Coastal Wandering

Walking a trail under the moonlight feels profoundly different than daytime hiking. Familiar paths take on new dimensions. The shadows lengthen while sounds travel farther and every step becomes more intentional.

In early evening hours, trails near Munro Trail and Hulopoe Bay on Lanai become accessible for safe exploration during full moons when natural illumination is optimal. The lowland paths that run close to Molokai's beaches along with short trails inside forested regions provide accessible hiking alternatives. Before setting out on a hike always monitor weather conditions and choose familiar paths while avoiding remote or rugged trails at night without professional guidance.

The journey itself holds importance rather than racing to a destination or summit. It's about listening. Noticing. The pace of movement must be gentle enough to allow one to hear wind rustling through trees and waves whispering from afar.

Hiking during nighttime turns into meditative journeys when combined with techniques such as breathwork or silent observation. Bring a small notebook. Maintain space to perceive with both vision and emotion.

Ocean Glow and Island Magic

During calm summer nights near certain coastlines you can observe the faint flickering light from bioluminescent plankton as waves brush across the sand. The appearance of this phenomenon is unpredictable and cannot be scheduled like a tour yet when it emerges it makes the ocean seem to come alive.

When you stand ankle-deep in the glowing surf with stars shining both above and below you feel as though you exist between two different skies. The most memorable experiences usually take place during late nights following long days when they occur unexpectedly. And they're never forgotten.

Cultural Experiences After Dark

The majority of organized cultural events occur during the day whereas the most personal gatherings on the island are held at night. Outdoor storytelling circles. Someone performs music beneath string lights in their backyard. During festival seasons the most vibrant evening activities include night markets and evening craft fairs.

Examine local community bulletin boards and inquire at your place of stay or speak with nearby merchants to find out about events. Approach these gatherings with respect because they are authentic community spaces rather than staged tourist attractions. A slack-key guitar performance captures your attention as you sit next to neighbors enjoying shared food and laughter while exchanging stories.

The most genuine experiences often remain completely off the tourist maps. They're offered.

Staying Safe and Present

Exploring at night requires extra awareness. Always inform someone about your hiking or stargazing plans when you plan to do it alone. Carry a flashlight or headlamp with spare batteries for nighttime activities. Choose sturdy footwear for protection and bring layered clothing while ensuring you do not stray from the designated paths.

During oceanfront evenings pay attention to tidal patterns and stay away from uncharted beaches after sunset.

The Gifts You Find When You Wander Differently

Some places don't reveal themselves at first glance. They wait. They ask for presence, for patience, for the kind of traveler who's willing to step off the itinerary and into the unknown.

The hidden gems of Lanai and Molokai aren't about secrecy or exclusivity. They're about stillness. About the chance to see the land as it really is—not polished or packaged, but real. They remind you that sometimes the most meaningful parts of a journey come when you're not trying to collect experiences, but when you're simply allowing them to find you.

A beach without footprints. A market that feels like a reunion. A tour that becomes a conversation. A night sky so vast it humbles the noise inside you. These aren't bucket list items. They're windows into a way of being that moves slower, listens more, and leaves room for awe.

You don't need a perfect plan to find these places. You just need curiosity. And a willingness to trust that what lies just beyond the beaten path might be the very thing you didn't know you were looking for.

So let yourself wander a little. Ask questions. Follow the turn in the trail. Say yes to something small. These islands have been waiting quietly, offering their beauty without demand. And if you meet them with open eyes and steady steps, they'll offer you something far more lasting than a postcard view.

They'll offer you a memory made of meaning—and a version of yourself that travels with more care.

Chapter Twelve

Safety and Practical Advice

The islands of Lanai and Molokai offer some of Hawaii's most serene, remote, and untouched landscapes. That serenity, however, doesn't negate the need for preparedness. Whether you're hiking forested trails or snorkeling offshore, safety begins before your feet hit the path—or the water.

Before any outdoor excursion, check the local weather forecast. Island weather is famously unpredictable, especially in upland areas where clouds gather quickly and sudden rain can turn trails muddy and streams dangerous to cross. If conditions shift, don't push it. There's no prize for finishing a hike in a downpour or paddling out into choppy waters.

Wearing the right gear is essential. For hikes, choose sturdy, closed-toe shoes with reliable grip—many trails involve uneven surfaces or rocky climbs. Bring sun protection: wide-brimmed hats, breathable long-sleeved shirts, and reef-safe sunscreen. For snorkeling, a properly fitted mask and fins make all the difference.

Skip anything flimsy or oversized—it's better to rent from a trusted local outfitter who can help you select the right size.

Hydration is critical. Always bring more water than you think you'll need, especially on longer hikes or warmer days. Dehydration happens fast in the tropical sun, and many trails lack natural shade or refill points.

Preparing for Outdoor Adventures

While Hawaii exudes a sense of welcome, it also operates on a foundation of respect—particularly when it comes to the land and sea. Some areas are protected, others are culturally sacred, and all are governed by specific state and local laws designed to preserve the environment and ensure public safety.

Fishing regulations are a prime example. Many shoreline and reef areas are governed by seasonal closures or permit requirements. Spearfishing, net use, and the taking of certain species are heavily monitored, especially around marine preserves. If you're unsure about a location, ask a local guide or check official state resources before casting a line.

Drone usage has also become a point of concern. As of recent legislation, drone fishing—using drones to drop bait or retrieve fish—is illegal in Hawaii. Additionally, drones are prohibited in many protected or sacred areas, including near heiau (temples), certain wildlife sanctuaries, and national parks. Always review local drone laws and adhere to FAA rules. In general, if you're unsure whether it's appropriate to fly, it probably isn't.

Risks to Be Aware Of

Even paradise has its hazards—many of them not immediately visible. Strong ocean currents, especially rip currents, are a leading danger for swimmers and snorkelers. These currents often occur near reef channels or around points where the shoreline curves inward. Always swim in designated areas when possible, and never ignore posted signs or lifeguard warnings. If you get caught in a rip current, stay calm—don't fight it. Swim parallel to shore until you're out of the current's grip.

Some hiking trails also carry risk due to steep drops, loose rocks, or sudden terrain changes. It's not uncommon to encounter narrow ledges or eroded sections, particularly on coastal cliff paths. Avoid venturing off marked trails, and if you're hiking alone, let someone know your route and expected return time.

Hawaii's natural beauty also includes some plants and animals best admired from a distance. Avoid contact with unfamiliar plants—some cause skin irritation or allergic reactions. And while it's rare to encounter anything dangerous in terms of wildlife, do give centipedes, jellyfish, and wild pigs a wide berth if you happen upon them.

In Case of Emergency

While Lanai and Molokai feel wonderfully remote, help is available if you need it. Each island has medical facilities and emergency services, but response times may vary depending on your location.

For **Lanai**:

- *Lanai Community Hospital* is the island's primary medical facility. Dial 911 for emergencies.

For **Molokai**:

- *Molokai General Hospital* in Kaunakakai offers full emergency services.

- For urgent needs, local clinics in town may offer faster access for minor issues.

In all cases:

- Dial **911** for life-threatening emergencies.

- Carry a basic first-aid kit, especially if you're heading into remote areas.

- Save local emergency numbers to your phone before you go offline.

Budgeting for Your Trip – What to Expect

Lanai and Molokai offer some of Hawaii's most enriching and authentic travel experiences—but like anywhere in the islands, they also come with a price tag. Because of their remote nature, limited infrastructure, and supply logistics, many things cost a bit more than you might expect. But with thoughtful planning and a few smart decisions, a trip here can remain both memorable and manageable.

Whether you're traveling solo, with a partner, or as a family, having a clear sense of what to expect financially can help you focus less on expenses—and more on the experience.

What You'll Likely Spend

Accommodations

On Lanai, prices tend to skew upscale. Luxury resorts and wellness retreats often start at $800 to $1,200 per night, especially during peak seasons. That said, a handful of mid-range guesthouses and vacation rentals can sometimes be found between $250 and $450 per night if booked early.

Molokai offers a broader range of affordable options. Family-owned inns, modest beach cottages, and vacation rentals typically range from $150 to $300 per night. These options may not come with valet service or pools, but they offer something arguably better: simplicity and connection.

Meals and Dining

Expect to spend around $15–$25 per person at casual eateries and food trucks. Sit-down meals at local restaurants may cost $30–$50 per person, depending on the location and what's in season. Groceries can also be more expensive than on the mainland, but if you have access to a kitchen, preparing a few of your own meals can significantly cut costs.

Transportation

Rental cars are limited, especially on Lanai, and can range from $90 to $150 per day. Be sure to reserve in advance. On Molokai, rates are similar, but vehicle availability is slightly more forgiving. Gasoline is generally more expensive on both islands.

Other options like bike rentals or shuttle services can be more budget-friendly, especially if you plan to stay close to one base.

Experiences and Excursions

Guided hikes, snorkel tours, or cultural workshops typically run $75 to $200 per person, depending on length and specialization. Some cultural activities, such as lei-making or taro patch volunteering, are offered at low or no cost, especially through community centers.

The Hidden Costs Most Visitors Miss

Resort Fees and Taxes

Many accommodations include additional resort fees—often $30 to $50 per night—for amenities like Wi-Fi, beach towels, or shuttle service. Hawaii's state and local taxes on lodging and purchases also add up quickly (currently 13–14% in most areas), so factor that into your nightly rates and meal expenses.

Tours and Equipment Add-Ons

Kayak, snorkel, or hiking equipment may not always be included in your excursion cost. Ask ahead of time whether gear is provided or needs to be rented separately. Also, keep an eye out for optional upgrades or gratuities that, while not mandatory, are customary and appreciated.

Connectivity and Convenience

Things like mobile data plans, cash-only businesses, or even ATM fees can sneak up on your budget. Always carry a little extra cash for roadside stands, small markets, or areas with spotty card service.

How to Stretch Your Budget Without Sacrificing Experience

Book Early, Travel Smart

The earlier you book your lodging, rental car, and inter-island transportation, the better your rates. Traveling in shoulder seasons (late spring or early fall) can also help you avoid peak pricing while still enjoying great weather and fewer crowds.

Plan Around Free or Low-Cost Activities

Some of the best things to do on Lanai and Molokai don't cost a thing. Hiking, beachcombing, visiting historical landmarks, or exploring tide pools offer powerful experiences without a price tag. Community-led events, markets, and festivals often include food, music, and cultural engagement for just a few dollars—or free.

Mix and Match Dining

Try balancing restaurant meals with simple picnics. Pick up fresh bread, fruit, and local cheese at the market, and enjoy a meal under a tree or by the water. You'll save money—and likely remember the setting more than the menu.

Tools and Resources to Help You Plan

Budgeting Apps and Trackers

Apps like Trail Wallet, TripCoin, or Mint can help you organize your travel budget in real time. Many allow you to set spending limits by category, helping you avoid surprises.

Local Deal Guides

Websites like *Hawaii Travel with Kids* or *Bank of Hawaii's blog* regularly publish updated money-saving tips, from local discounts to seasonal deals. These resources can uncover lesser-known savings opportunities on both islands.

Community Advice

Ask locals. Hotel staff, shopkeepers, and market vendors often know about events, places, or tips you won't find in guidebooks. Something as simple as asking "What would you do with $20 on the island?" can lead to an unforgettable (and affordable) experience.

Planning your finances ahead of time doesn't have to be restrictive—it can actually make your time here feel more spacious. When you know what to expect and where to flex, you'll move through your trip with confidence and ease.

The islands will meet you with beauty, no matter your budget.

Avoiding Tourist Traps – Genuine Experiences

Even on the quieter islands of Lanai and Molokai, it's possible to encounter experiences designed more for profit than authenticity. While the scale is smaller than on Oahu or Maui, tourist traps can still sneak into your itinerary—usually in the form of overpriced shops, crowded sightseeing stops, or activities that feel more scripted than sincere.

The key isn't to avoid all popular experiences. Some are beloved for good reason. The goal is to spot when something's been stripped of its meaning and repackaged for convenience. Because when you come all this way, what you deserve is something real.

Common Tourist Traps to Avoid

Be cautious around locations that are heavily advertised but lack depth. These may include souvenir-heavy roadside stops with inflated prices, commercial luaus that feel more like stage productions than cultural events, or viewpoints packed with selfie stations and little context.

If something seems unusually polished, ask yourself: who is this for? If the experience feels more focused on spectacle than story, it may not be the best use of your time—or your money.

Whether it's vendors pushing shell necklaces at marked-up prices or "exclusive" excursion packages being promoted at your hotel, it's wise to take a breath before buying. These offerings are often targeted at travelers with limited time who are eager to make the most of it. But higher prices don't always equal better experiences.

A good rule of thumb: if the offer comes with urgency or pressure, it's okay to step away.

Finally, it's important to keep in mind that not all gift stores are created equal. Many carry mass-produced items made outside of Hawaii, even if they're decorated with island imagery. These shops often advertise "Hawaiian gifts" but sell products that have no actual connection to local artists or communities.

Look for items with tags that indicate local sourcing, or ask who made it. If the staff can't tell you, that's usually your answer.

Finding the Real Hawaii

Skip the hotel buffet. Instead, head to a food truck, a family-run lunch counter, or a beachside market. Ask locals where they go for poke, plate lunch, or fresh fruit. You'll not only pay less—you'll taste more. In many cases, the person serving you has also grown, caught, or prepared the meal.

Markets, craft fairs, festivals, and even church fundraisers can be incredible windows into local life. These aren't curated for tourists—they're created for residents. You'll meet artisans selling their own work, musicians playing for friends, and aunties serving homemade desserts from coolers under a tent.

These are the places where generosity is genuine, and you'll often be welcomed with warmth—especially if you show sincere interest and respect.

If you're looking to explore hula, lei-making, or traditional farming, avoid any experience that feels packaged. Instead, seek out workshops offered through cultural centers, nonprofit organizations, or schools. These programs are usually taught by people who practice what they teach—and share it because they care, not because it's profitable.

Tips for Spotting a Tourist Trap

Check reviews: If an experience is described as "great for Instagram" more than it's described for its depth or meaning, be wary.

Look for signs of rushed timing: Tours that move quickly through multiple locations often favor efficiency over depth.

Notice who else is there: If the crowd is entirely tourists and there's no local participation, the experience may not reflect the true culture.

Ask questions: Where are the products made? Who leads the tour? What's included in the cost? Genuine operations will answer transparently.

Stories from the Other Side

One traveler on Molokai skipped a promoted "island sampler" tour and instead struck up a conversation with a farmer at a small produce stand. That chat turned into an invitation to visit the farm later in the week—where she not only toured the property, but shared a home-cooked lunch and learned the story behind each ingredient.

Another guest on Lanai chose to attend a free hula demonstration at a community center rather than book a theatrical luau. He left not with a cocktail in a pineapple, but with a deep understanding of what the dance meant—and how long it takes to learn even the first verse.

These moments don't always show up in travel brochures. But they're the ones that stay with you.

Health and Wellbeing – Staying Fit and Relaxed

Travel often challenges routines—but it also offers a unique opportunity to reconnect with your body, your energy, and your surroundings. On Lanai and Molokai, wellness isn't a service—it's a setting. Here, you don't need a spa day to feel restored. Sometimes all it takes is a walk at sunrise, a barefoot stretch in the sand, or a deep breath under a canopy of stars.

That said, there are plenty of ways to stay fit and well during your trip—both formally and informally. The key is to listen to what your body needs, and to engage with the islands in ways that nourish rather than deplete.

Keep Moving, Gently

You don't need a gym to stay active in Hawaii. Morning beach runs, shoreline walks, or ocean swims are all excellent ways to start the day. Lanai's cooler uplands make it ideal for hiking, while Molokai's open stretches invite bike rides and nature walks. Many of these activities don't require gear or reservations—just a willingness to get outside.

If you're craving something more structured, beach yoga classes are available on both islands, often hosted by wellness centers or resort programs. Some are donation-based or open to the public, especially around sunrise or sunset.

Want to feel like a local while working up a sweat? Look for drop-in volleyball games at public parks, tai chi sessions at community centers, or fitness classes posted on bulletin boards in small towns. These gatherings are less about performance and more about community—showing up is enough.

Make Time for Restoration

For a deeper reset, several resorts and independent wellness studios offer full-body treatments rooted in traditional Hawaiian healing practices. Lomilomi massage, for instance, is more than physical therapy—it's spiritual realignment through rhythm and breath. Treatments often include native plants, oils, and chants designed to connect body and mind.

Molokai's retreats tend to be more rustic and community-based, while Lanai offers more luxurious options, including dedicated wellness resorts like Sensei Lānaʻi, which integrate technology, mindfulness, and movement.

Whether guided or solo, the environment on these islands lends itself to mindfulness. Ocean sounds, forest trails, and even open-air lanais (porches) are natural places to pause and reset. You might not find daily meditation sessions unless you're staying at a retreat center—but you can always create your own moment of stillness.

Try sitting quietly at a scenic overlook. Close your eyes. Count your breaths. It doesn't have to be long or formal. It just has to be yours.

Staying Healthy While Traveling

The Hawaiian sun is beautiful—but it's strong. Dehydration can sneak up quickly, especially on long hikes or days spent in the ocean. Drink more water than you think you need, and keep a refillable bottle with you at all times. Many parks, markets, and even beaches now offer refill stations.

Food-wise, it's easy to stay on track if you lean into local offerings. Tropical fruits like papaya, mango, and pineapple are abundant, and plate lunches often include generous servings of rice, fish, and vegetables. If you're eating out frequently, balance heavier meals with lighter ones, and aim to include at least one fresh or raw item at each meal.

If you have dietary needs or allergies, many restaurants are accommodating—just ask. You'll find that "fresh" is a common theme here, which helps support healthier choices without much effort.

Hawaii's time zone may feel disorienting at first, especially if you've come from the mainland U.S. or farther abroad. To adjust more easily:

- Get outside in natural light during the day.

- Avoid naps longer than 30 minutes.

- Eat meals at local times.

- Try light stretching or a short walk before bed to ease into sleep.

If you're traveling with children or arriving late at night, plan for a buffer day. Don't schedule anything ambitious until your body catches up to your location.

Dealing with Minor Health Concerns

No one wants to think about illness or injury on vacation—but having a plan makes any bump in the road feel manageable.

Pack a small travel health kit: bandages, antiseptic wipes, electrolyte packets, and over-the-counter medications for things like motion sickness or stomach upset. Include insect repellent and reef-safe sunscreen—both essential on the islands.

For anything more serious, each island has a hospital or urgent care clinic. Know where the closest one is located, and save the number in your phone before heading out. Pharmacies are also available in central towns, and many hotel front desks keep basic supplies on hand.

If you're snorkeling, hiking, or doing water sports, make sure your travel insurance covers these activities—just in case.

A Healthy Trip Is a Present One

Staying well on the road isn't about sticking to a rigid routine. It's about being aware, being adaptable, and taking care of the body that's carrying you through this experience. In Lanai and Molokai, wellness happens naturally when you slow down, listen, and let the land lead.

So stretch. Hydrate. Rest. Laugh. Walk barefoot. Choose the trail that calls to you, and take your time getting there. Wellness isn't found in a schedule—it's found in how you feel when the day ends and you realize: you showed up fully.

Moving Through the Islands with Care

Being safe doesn't mean being afraid. It means being present.

In Lanai and Molokai, safety is less about guardrails and more about awareness. It's knowing where you're stepping, when the tide shifts, how the sun feels at midday, and what local customs ask of you. It's the simple wisdom of preparing well so you can explore freely.

Staying healthy, budgeting wisely, avoiding the noise of commercial tourism—these aren't just strategies for smoother travel. They're acts of respect. For the place. For the people. And for yourself.

Chapter Thirteen

Sustainability and Responsible Travel

S ustainability isn't a checklist. It's a mindset. A way of moving through the world that asks not just where you're going, but how—and what you leave behind.

On Lanai and Molokai, where the rhythms of land and sea are deeply felt and easily disrupted, the stakes of travel are more visible. These islands don't just invite us to admire nature—they challenge us to travel in ways that protect it.

The good news? Sustainable travel isn't complicated. It's made up of small, thoughtful decisions. Choices that, over time and in numbers, make a difference.

Start With How You Move

One of the simplest ways to reduce your environmental impact is to rethink transportation. On islands with limited roadways and compact communities, the need for a rental car often fades after arrival.

Whenever possible, choose to walk or bike—not just because it's greener, but because it slows you down. You notice more. You interact more. And you become part of the place rather than passing through it.

When longer distances are involved, shared shuttle services or carpool-friendly tours help reduce emissions while supporting local operators. If you do rent a vehicle, opt for a hybrid or electric model when available, and combine errands or excursions to minimize overall mileage.

Sustainability begins with movement. Not just where you go—but how lightly you get there.

Where You Stay Matters

Accommodations are another powerful point of impact. Many travelers now choose lodgings that operate with eco-certifications or green infrastructure—but even without official labels, some of the most sustainable places to stay are small, locally owned inns that reflect environmental care in quieter ways.

Look for places that:

- Use solar or renewable energy sources
- Provide natural ventilation in place of excessive air conditioning
- Offer filtered water refill stations to reduce plastic waste
- Compost or source food from nearby farms

Choosing to support such places means your dollars stay closer to the community—and your stay leaves a softer imprint.

The Power of Reusables

In remote areas, even the simplest habits matter. A plastic bottle tossed in a trash bin doesn't just disappear—it often stays on the island, sometimes on the shoreline. One of the easiest ways to reduce waste is to travel with your own reusable water bottle, utensils, and shopping bag.

Many cafes, markets, and food trucks on the islands appreciate when visitors come prepared. It shows care. It starts conversations. And it quietly helps build a culture where sustainability becomes the norm, not the exception.

Consider going one step further by packing:

- A foldable tote for market days
- A collapsible container for leftovers
- A metal or bamboo straw for drinks on the go

They take up little space in your bag—but the impact is lasting.

Eat with Intention

Sustainability extends to the plate. Choosing to dine at local restaurants that source from island farms or fisheries reduces your foodprint and supports people who are working with, not against, the land.

Seek out menus that feature:

- Line-caught or reef-safe seafood
- Taro, ulu (breadfruit), or kalo, grown traditionally
- Organic produce sourced from nearby valleys or upland farms

You don't have to give up flavor or comfort—if anything, you gain deeper connection. Food becomes a story. A form of place-based learning. A way to experience the island through its seasons and soil.

Conserving Energy, Even When You're Not Home

Sustainability isn't only about what you do out in the world—it's also about how you exist in a space.

When staying anywhere, adopt the same mindful habits you would at home:

- Turn off lights and ceiling fans when leaving a room
- Unplug electronics that aren't in use
- Limit air conditioning by opening windows or using natural shade
- Take shorter showers to conserve water—especially during dry seasons

These aren't burdens. They're small expressions of respect. And on islands where utilities are precious and often imported, even the smallest changes carry weight.

Collective Impact, One Choice at a Time

When we talk about sustainability, it's easy to feel overwhelmed. But the truth is, every footprint is made one step at a time. No traveler gets it perfect. What matters is choosing to care—and acting on that care in ways that are honest, imperfect, and real.

Lanai and Molokai don't need visitors to be experts. They just need them to be attentive. To understand that sustainability isn't a separate category of travel. It's travel done right.

And it starts not with guilt or pressure—but with a simple question: How can I give more than I take

Supporting Local Communities

The unique atmosphere of Molokai becomes evident during your first hours on the island. When visiting Lanai you may require a day before you sense it but it exists nonetheless. You have the feeling of being part of something bigger than just an isolated island. You're stepping into a living, breathing community.

In regions where tourism meets tradition while family roots remain strong and land represents more than just scenery, your approach to visiting holds significant importance. Responsible tourism should go beyond the mere act of checking a box when supporting local communities. Your presence should match the ongoing life of a place which remains unchanged when you depart.

Show Up With Intention, Not Just Curiosity

Start with the mindset. Responsible travel starts when you explore a place by listening as well as seeing. Approaching every experience with both curiosity and humility allows you to fully engage and respect the present moment.

Make it a point to participate in local events by joining as an invited guest rather than a mere observer. Ask questions with care. Observe cultural customs before joining in. Visitors receive welcome access to festivals, farm tours, or storytelling nights but their participation will either strengthen or weaken their welcome.

When someone invites you to share food, express your thanks through acceptance. When someone shares their story with you, value it as if it were a precious gift rather than just another soundbite.

Volunteer and Contribute Where It Counts

Travelers can contribute to conservation programs and nonprofit groups across the islands through short-term volunteer opportunities instead of financial donations. Your day could start with native plant restoration on a hillside or beach cleanup following a storm.

These aren't grand gestures—but they're meaningful. Through your actions you demonstrate a commitment to the islands' future while you enjoy their natural beauty. Your presence alone often stands as the greatest contribution you can make when help is needed.

Respect Cultural Boundaries and Traditions

Responsible tourism requires the recognition that certain destinations should remain exclusive and some cultural practices should remain unique to local communities.

Visitors must understand that sacred sites along with traditional ceremonies and specific ecological zones might be inaccessible or subject to particular entry conditions. It's not a denial of access. It's a preservation of balance.

Follow posted guidelines. Stay on marked paths. When you're uncertain about whether photography is allowed ask for permission. Understand a negative response about recording as permission to observe without capturing the moment. To be present, rather than collecting.

Understanding cultural respect requires living with awareness and letting reverence guide your actions through the world.

Choose Local, Every Time

Where your money goes, your impact follows. When you support local businesses you are investing in family livelihoods instead of corporate profits. It represents support for maintaining unique island characteristics despite worldwide uniformity.

Shopping at farmers markets should be about forming connections instead of just buying souvenirs. Stay in locally run inns and guesthouses. Choose to dine at restaurants that source food from local farms while employing nearby residents.

Ask about the owners of a tour company when making your travel arrangements. Always find out the origin of the products you purchase. Through these brief exchanges you demonstrate your awareness of the individuals providing service and show that your decision to be there represents deliberate support for them.

Minor spending decisions generate long-lasting impacts through their ripple effects. A jar of locally made honey. A hand-carved ornament. Traditional design patterns are printed on this fabric piece. These aren't just mementos. They're acts of support.

Long-Term Impact: Beyond the Visit

Properly executed tourism extends its impact beyond mere physical traces. It leaves a positive legacy.

Responsible tourism provides financial support for cultural preservation and educational programs while financing infrastructure improvements that serve the entire community. Tourism generates home-based employment opportunities for local residents. The establishment of culturally relevant jobs motivates young locals to choose professions which honor their historical roots and natural surroundings.

The most essential benefit of tourism lies in its ability to establish mutual understanding between different people. This approach to understanding works to eliminate stereotypes through mutual storytelling.

When travelers connect with local communities they experience lasting changes in their lives because of the people who welcomed them into their world rather than just their visual experiences. The transformation experienced during numerous visits collectively establishes a sustainable and respectful long-term travel culture.

Being a Good Guest

Each culture establishes specific rules for welcoming visitors. The Aloha Spirit in Hawaii represents a dual approach to welcoming and connecting people from different backgrounds.

Approaching your visit with openness, care and a gentle presence will ensure you are seen as more than just a tourist. Your presence will reflect an understanding of temporary participation in something meaningful.

This type of travel benefits others more than it benefits the traveler.

Bringing Home a Piece of Hawaii Sustainably

What you bring home from a journey says a lot about how you traveled.

In places like Lanai and Molokai—where craftsmanship is intimate, and culture is lived rather than displayed—souvenirs aren't just about memory. They're about support, preservation, and relationship. A meaningful souvenir honors not just the beauty of the islands, but the hands and hearts that shaped it.

Sustainable shopping isn't about avoiding mementos. It's about choosing ones that carry story and soul.

Handmade Not the Mass-Produced

The easiest way to spot a sustainable souvenir is to look for signs of human touch. Was it made locally? Is the artist's name attached? Can you speak to the person who created it—or at least learn their story?

Many artisans on Molokai and Lanai sell directly through community markets, cooperative galleries, or local shops. You'll find:

- Woven lauhala goods like bracelets, mats, and fans
- Traditional quilts with symbolic designs passed down through generations
- Shell jewelry made from responsibly collected beach finds
- Wood carvings or prints inspired by island flora and fauna

These items don't just reflect island aesthetics—they carry cultural meaning. When you choose handmade over factory-made, you're investing in tradition, not trend.

Choose Materials that Respect the Land

Sustainability isn't just about where something was made—but what it's made from. The best souvenirs are crafted from natural, renewable, or recycled materials that minimize harm to the environment.

Look for products made from:

- Recycled glass or metals
- Coconut shells, bamboo, or driftwood
- Natural dyes from native plants
- Organic cotton, kapa, or reclaimed fabric

Avoid items made from coral, exotic woods, or animal parts—even if legally sold. Just because something's available doesn't mean it's appropriate. Ask yourself: would the island benefit from me taking this home?

And when in doubt, don't hesitate to ask vendors where their materials come from. Sustainable makers are often proud to share their sourcing practices.

Let Food Tell the Story

Some of the most heartfelt souvenirs are meant to be eaten or shared. Locally produced goods let you bring a piece of the island's flavor home with you—and support small farms and food producers in the process.

Consider packing:

- Jars of locally harvested honey
- Sea salt blends with native herbs
- Tropical fruit jams or dried mango
- Roasted coffee from island-grown beans

These items are often made in small batches, using ingredients grown just miles from where they're sold. They don't just taste good—they support local food systems and reduce reliance on imported goods.

When shopping, check for minimal packaging and reusable or recyclable containers. Many island producers have embraced compostable wrapping, glass jars, or low-waste alternatives.

Support Artists Who Preserve Culture

Some souvenirs hold more than aesthetic value—they carry living history. Artists who work with traditional Hawaiian methods, tools, or symbolism are helping preserve identity in the face of change.

When you purchase from these artists, you're not just buying a product. You're helping keep a lineage alive.

These pieces might include:

- Story quilts with embedded generational meaning
- Reproductions of petroglyph-inspired carvings
- Contemporary art rooted in ancestral practices

If a piece feels expensive, ask why. Often, you're paying for time, training, and cultural significance—not just materials. And that price helps sustain a practice that might otherwise fade.

Know What to Avoid

Even well-meaning travelers can unintentionally purchase items that undermine local culture or harm ecosystems. As a general rule, avoid:

- Anything mass-produced and labeled "Hawaiian" without cultural context

- Items made overseas but sold in tourist shops
- Products featuring sacred symbols without explanation or origin
- Shells, rocks, or sand collected from natural environments
- Coral jewelry or accessories made from endangered species

When souvenirs are stripped of origin or meaning, they become decoration. But when they're chosen with care, they become connection.

A New Way to Remember

The best souvenirs aren't the most eye-catching. They're the ones that make you pause when you see them later—the ones that carry a conversation, a scent, a smile from the person who handed them to you.

They remind you not just where you went, but how you moved through the place. What you learned. What you valued.

Sustainable souvenirs aren't about less. They're about more meaning, more connection, and more integrity.

So when you choose what to carry home, ask: does this item honor the place it came from? Does it reflect the kind of traveler I want to be?

If the answer is yes, you're not just taking a memory—you're carrying a piece of the island's heart.

Embracing Change and Conservation

Travel has always changed us. The current request requires us to allow travel to transform us.

These two Hawaiian islands sit at an intersection where preservation conflicts with pressure while tradition battles tourism and resilience faces risk. Our travel decisions in these delicate and holy environments extend beyond individual preferences. They're part of a global story.

Innovation That Honors the Land

Emerging developments across islands are transforming travel operations while safeguarding essential elements. Eco-friendly travel solutions such as solar-powered accommodations and low-emission ferries alongside indigenous trail restoration projects illustrate this industry transformation. Travelers now experience locations through intelligent and environmentally friendly methods.

Renewable energy has moved beyond fringe ideas and become mainstream. It's becoming central to how tourism operates. Travelers help shape tourism by choosing businesses that share this sustainable vision.

Eco-tourism is also evolving. The eco-tourism industry now extends beyond hiking activities and "green" branding strategies. Immersive education-based experiences enable travelers to understand how they should act as guests of the land rather than just visitors.

More guides today create experiences that merge ecological science and cultural history through coastal reef monitoring tours and native reforestation hikes to provide meaningful and restorative experiences.

Technology With a Purpose

Conservation efforts become significantly stronger when technology is used with purposeful intent.

Drones and wildlife trackers allow researchers to study endangered species without disturbing their natural habitats. Satellite imaging supports watershed preservation. Ordinary travel apps currently provide functionality for tracking carbon footprints while optimizing travel routes and notifying users about nearby sustainable choices.

Travelers receive updated details about weather effects and trail shutdowns while discovering sustainable tour options. This development creates an opportunity for intentional travel planning.

Prior to your departure you can evaluate your estimated emissions and select reputable programs to offset them. During your stay you can monitor your energy usage and water consumption levels. Travelers have the opportunity to engage with communities that prioritize regenerative travel practices which focus on restoration alongside reduction.

Be an Agent of Change

Inspiring change requires no platform because your practice alone can make a difference. You just need practice. Share what you learn. Talk about your choices with fellow travelers. Low-waste habits and local-first spending strategies prove not only achievable but also offer significant rewards.

Speak up. Leave reviews for eco-conscious businesses. Choose guides who protect heritage rather than taking advantage of it. Help direct others toward better options.

Stay curious. As you gain knowledge about a location you become less likely to overlook its value. You become more inclined to experience travel with humility.

A Vision of Travel That Heals

It's easy to focus on what's being lost: coral bleaching, cultural erosion, overcrowded destinations. But the future of travel isn't doomed. The tourism landscape is undergoing a transformation through community boundary establishment and business model changes together with travelers opting for meaningful experiences instead of numerous visits.

This future isn't theoretical. Quiet conversations with small policy adjustments and grassroots movements show it is already progressing. But it needs momentum. The movement requires tourists who seek experiences deeper than postcards and packing lists.

It needs people like you.

Leaving It Better

The best travel experiences provide more than just rest and inspiration. They leave you more responsible and more awake to your impact. You become more conscious of how you can contribute to something greater than your individual existence.

As you walk these islands, ask yourself: Do my actions as a traveler improve this place or do they simply increase its visitor count?

That question alone changes everything.

Caring travel leads to a future that goes beyond sustainability. It's full of possibilities.

Traveling Light, Leaving Meaning

It's one thing to admire a place. It's another to protect it.

Sustainable travel isn't about getting everything right. It's about choosing to care—consistently, humbly, and in ways that ripple beyond your own itinerary. In places like Lanai and Molokai, where the line between community and environment is beautifully blurred, the invitation is simple: Travel like you belong to something.

Belonging doesn't mean ownership. It means relationship. It means seeing that your choices—what you carry, where you stay, how you eat, what you take home—aren't isolated. They echo.

You may never meet the farmer who grew the fruit you bought at a roadside stand. You might not see the sapling you helped plant grow into a shade tree. But somewhere, quietly, your presence shaped something.

And that's the kind of legacy that matters.

These islands don't need perfect visitors. They need present ones. People willing to learn, to slow down, and to give back more than they take.

So as your journey continues, whether on these shores or elsewhere, carry this with you: Sustainability isn't a limit. It's an invitation—to move with care, to act with respect, and to leave a trail of connection instead of consumption.

In doing so, you're not just traveling differently.

You're helping the world stay beautifully, meaningfully intact.

Chapter Fourteen

Visual Storytelling and Photography

Capturing Landscapes — Techniques and Tips

There's a particular kind of stillness that lives in the landscapes of Lanai and Molokai. It isn't passive. It holds presence. As a traveler, you might try to describe it with words, but sometimes, the lens says it better. Photography becomes more than documentation here—it becomes a form of reverence.

To capture these islands well, you don't need the latest camera body or the most expensive lens. What you need is a willingness to pause. To observe. To understand that the light, the land, and the line between them are telling a story—and you're simply listening with your eyes.

Light, Lines, and Layers

The first thing you learn when photographing landscapes is that the land itself is never static. Clouds shift. Shadows stretch. Colors bloom and fade depending on the time of day. And nowhere is this more true than in Hawaii, where sun, sea, and sky constantly reshape the view.

One of the most powerful tools in a landscape photographer's kit is leading lines. Whether it's a winding trail through red dirt cliffs or a shoreline that disappears into horizon mist, a strong line invites the viewer into the frame. Lanai's Munro Trail offers opportunities to use tree-lined ridges or descending switchbacks to draw the eye through the image. On Molokai, the coast near Halawa Valley provides natural curvature in both land and water—perfect for visual storytelling.

Incorporating foreground elements is another way to create depth. A lava rock, a flower, a lone tree leaning into the breeze—these anchors help balance the vastness of ocean or sky. Without them, images can feel flat or distant. But with the right foreground, you place the viewer inside the scene, not just in front of it.

More Than a Setting

Light isn't just a technical consideration—it's the mood-setter, the frame-shaper, the soul of the photograph.

On Lanai and Molokai, the golden hour—that window just after sunrise and before sunset—is especially magical. The low angle of the sun casts long shadows, warms the colors of the earth, and adds a softness that makes even the roughest terrain feel touchable. The orange glow across the Garden of the Gods at sunset, or the soft, diffused light at dawn as it filters through mist in Molokai's mountains, can turn an ordinary shot into something sacred.

Harsh midday light, by contrast, is often avoided—but not always. Sometimes, it reveals the stark contrast between shade and sun, bringing out the rugged texture of rocks or the pure shimmer of the ocean. If you shoot during these hours, consider converting your images to black and white. What you lose in color, you gain in contrast and shape.

Composition that Invites Curiosity

Good composition is about balance, not symmetry. It's about leading the eye and leaving space for imagination.

The rule of thirds remains one of the most effective techniques. Imagine dividing your image into nine equal parts—three across, three down. Placing key elements (like the horizon or a tree) along these lines or at their intersections helps create visual tension and interest. On Molokai, placing the sea at the bottom third and a distant ridge along the top third creates both space and focus. On Lanai, a lone hiker positioned off-center on a ridgeline creates a sense of movement and scale.

Natural framing also works beautifully. Use overhanging branches, rock archways, or even the curve of a trail to frame the scene. It draws the viewer's gaze inward while giving context to the shot. Think of it as an invitation—one that says, "Come see what I saw."

Breaking the Rules with Intention

Once you understand the rules, you're free to break them—but only with purpose. Lanai and Molokai are perfect places to experiment because their landscapes reward curiosity.

Long exposure photography is especially powerful near water. By slowing your shutter speed, you can transform crashing waves into smooth, misty textures that feel dreamlike. This works beautifully at Shipwreck Beach, where the movement of the sea contrasts with the stillness of the rusted ship in the distance.

Reflections also offer creative opportunities. Look for still water after rain or tide pools at low tide. A single palm tree mirrored in a quiet pool can feel more profound than a wide-angle vista.

Don't be afraid to get low. Or to shoot into the sun. Or to capture something imperfect—a crooked tree, a crumbling wall, a trail worn with use. Perfection isn't the goal. Presence is.

Practicing Visual Restraint

Some moments aren't meant to be photographed. That may sound strange in a chapter about photography, but it's true. There will be times when the light is right, the frame is set, and the scene is unfolding in front of you—but lifting your camera would take you out of the experience.

Knowing when to put the camera down is just as important as knowing when to pick it up. Respect ceremonies. Read the room at community gatherings. Watch how locals interact with the land and mirror their pace. Sometimes the best images are the ones you never take but that live in memory with the clarity only quiet can preserve.

Photographing Local Life — Candid Moments

If landscapes reveal the soul of a place, then its people reveal its heartbeat. On Lanai and Molokai, everyday moments unfold with an honesty that rarely asks for attention. A fisherman repairs his net in the shade. A grandmother teaches her grandchild to dance hula on a breezy porch. Locals gather at a market stand, trading laughter over fresh fruit. These are the quiet, unscripted rhythms of island life—and when captured thoughtfully, they become visual stories far richer than staged portraits ever could.

Candid photography isn't just a technique. It's a way of seeing. One that invites humility, patience, and the willingness to wait for life to speak on its own terms.

How to Become Part of the Scene

The best candid photographers don't stand out. They don't direct or stage. They blend into the background like a stone in a stream, allowing the world to flow naturally around them.

On these islands, that might mean spending time without your camera in hand—just walking through a town, browsing a market, or sitting on a bench near the harbor. When people stop noticing you as an observer, that's when real moments begin to emerge.

Using smaller, less conspicuous gear can also help. A lightweight mirrorless camera or even a high-quality phone camera lets you move freely and shoot without drawing too much attention. Turn off shutter sounds. Avoid long lenses that create distance. Be near. Be present.

And most importantly—be respectful. Not every moment is yours to capture.

The Ethics of Everyday Photography

In some cases, it's obvious when you should ask permission. If you're pointing your camera directly at someone, especially during an intimate or cultural moment, it's only right to ask first. A smile, a small wave, or a quiet question can go a long way. Many locals are happy to share a moment if you approach with sincerity.

But some candid shots unfold at a distance, with no clear interaction. In those cases, let your own sense of respect be your guide. Would you want to be photographed in that moment? Is the image about admiration—or intrusion?

On Molokai especially, cultural sensitivity is deeply rooted. There's a reason many locals say this island is not for tourists but for guests. Carrying a camera doesn't change that. Your presence is a responsibility.

If someone asks not to be photographed—or even seems uncomfortable—put the camera down. No image is worth the cost of trust.

Festivals, Markets, and Moments in Motion

Events like community festivals or farmers' markets offer rich opportunities for candid photography. There's energy, movement, color, and tradition—all in one space. But navigating these places with a camera requires grace.

Try to position yourself on the edge of activity rather than in the middle of it. Use natural cover—shade from a tent, the corner of a booth—to observe without interrupting. Capture interactions, not just expressions. A handshake, a shared laugh, a gesture across generations—these are the images that tell deeper stories.

At larger events like hula performances or holiday celebrations, consider photographing the atmosphere rather than the performers. The crowd's reaction. The child is watching with wide eyes. The grandmother is tapping her foot to the rhythm. These are the frames that offer cultural context without commodifying tradition.

Building a Visual Narrative

One photo can capture a moment. A sequence of photos can tell a story.

Think about how your images might flow together—not just as standalone shots, but as parts of a visual arc. Start wide to establish context, then move closer. Show the environment, then the people within it, then the intimate details—the clasped hands, the worn fishing net, the flower tucked behind an ear.

Use contrast and variation. Mix stillness with motion. Pair quiet portraits with wider crowd shots. Layer light and shadow. Let your collection breathe like a story with chapters.

And remember: stories don't have to be dramatic. Sometimes the most powerful narrative is simply that life is unfolding, unfiltered and unposed.

The Best Times and Places for Sunset Shots

Sunsets in Hawaii aren't just endings. They're transitions. The slow and radiant transitions of sunset teach us to experience time through feelings rather than control it. As night falls on Lanai and Molokai, the sky transitions without crowds or flashes. The event unfolds quietly while visitors mostly remain silent throughout.

Capturing these moments requires technical expertise but also demands patience and awareness while allowing photographers to sense feelings before they emerge. The process starts by determining both your location and the right moment to pause.

Where to Watch the Light Fall

Viewers can experience some of the most stunning twilight displays from the southern coast of Lanai. The volcanic cliffs framing calm waters make Hulopoe Bay a well-deserved favorite destination. The entire bay begins to shimmer with rose gold and soft lavender as the sun moves closer to the horizon. When you stand on the beach, you can capture both the ocean and sky using gentle foreground features like curved palm trunks and tide pools or lava rocks that break the surface.

Trails ascending from the bay provide an elevated viewing point for better perspective. The coastline curves while multicolored layers develop in the background.

Papohaku Beach on Molokai presents a distinctive form of natural spectacle. This beach stretches over three miles of uninterrupted sand and offers a clear view of the sunset descending into the ocean. The expansive area creates room for broad cinematic captures that reveal the western shore's stunning isolation and natural beauty.

The rugged terrain near the eastern sea cliffs frames sunsets while ocean mist rises and coastal tree silhouettes provide depth and texture to the scene. These spots receive few visitors and are set far from bustling areas, providing peaceful settings that create excellent conditions for intimate filming sessions.

Arrive Early, Stay Late

A frequent error during sunset photography includes photographers reaching their location just when the sun reaches the horizon. The enchanting experience starts before the sun sets and remains after it goes down.

Position yourself at least thirty minutes before sunset to prepare your frame while adjusting settings and observing light changes. You will see clouds that pick up colors during early stages, and you will observe reflections appearing in tide pools. The best photographic compositions usually develop during the moments leading up to the official "golden moment."

Wait until after sunset has finished before starting to pack away your equipment. The period after sunset, known as the blue hour, turns landscapes into shades of deep indigo with delicate purple tones along with silvery highlights. Long exposure photography becomes effective during these times when subtle light transforms into artistic effects.

The sky's transformation shows you how to pause and appreciate each moment. The experience of watching the sky transform becomes another element of the story.

Composing the Moment

Creating an outstanding sunset photograph requires more than vibrant colors. It's about structure, scale, and emotion.

Implement the rule of thirds to maintain a balanced horizon line by setting it in the lower third when the sky dominates the image and in the upper third when foreground elements are the main point of interest. Silhouettes make powerful anchors in sunset compositions. The softness of the sky finds its contrast in the presence of a single tree, a person standing upright, or jagged rocks rising from the ground.

Images gain depth from textures found in the foreground, including footprints in sand and rocky shorelines. Capture images from a low angle or move back to ensure the full environment narrates the scene.

The presence of water transforms reflections into an additional canvas for your image. Calm conditions can mirror the sky perfectly. Slight ripples add texture. Arrange your position to allow the reflection to complement rather than dominate the original scene.

Playing with Exposure and Atmosphere

Small exposure adjustments improve the quality of sunset photographs. Slightly underexposing your shot by half to a full stop maintains color saturation while preventing blown-out highlights. This approach strengthens silhouette visibility while making reds and oranges appear more vibrant.

Extend exposure time with a tripod and slow shutter speed to achieve smooth water reflections or capture cloud movement. When using a neutral density filter, you can achieve longer exposure times, which is particularly useful while shooting before complete darkness sets in.

Even handheld, you can capture remarkable atmosphere. Let shadows creep in. Introduce slight grain into your image. Mood matters more than perfection.

The Moment Before the Memory

Sunsets are both a gift and a goodbye. They encourage you to reduce your pace while prompting you to observe for extended periods before departing. Taking their photographs requires focused attention because it demands deliberate stillness instead of distraction.

The unmarked occasions of beauty on Lanai and Molokai occur naturally without any ceremonies. There are no rows of tripods. No cheers when the sun disappears. You, along with the light and the land, stand alone as you capture each moment through your camera's shutter.

The simplicity and honesty of your images from these locations allow them to stay with you long after sunset.

Sharing Your Story

Taking a photo is one thing. The act of sharing an image means providing context and emotion, which creates a distinct experience. The era of social media metrics makes it tempting to write travel narratives meant to captivate audiences. The most long-lasting travel stories emerge out of authenticity rather than perfection. They come from presence.

The islands of Lanai and Molokai exist beyond our need to display them. They invite connection. The places want you to experience them through your eyes before you describe them with your words. When you opt to share your experiences through writing or visual content on social media platforms, your focus should be on expressing a personal connection rather than promoting a destination.

Crafting a Narrative That Resonates

Captivating travel content develops from experiences rather than starting with photography. The most captivating travel content starts with a single moment, such as an insight or a conversation that changes how you see things. Start there.

Blog entries and photo captions need to demonstrate an arc to be effective posts. Begin with a setting or feeling. Lead with either a probing question or an intriguing detail to captivate your readers from the start. Take your readers along as you navigate the hike and meal, encounter strangers, and embrace the quiet moments. Finish your piece with reflection instead of a summary.

A simple construction doesn't require extended length or complicated elements. A short caption can hold significant power when it reflects reality. "I thought I came here for solitude. I discovered a community connection while sitting on a porch in Molokai.

Matching Message to Platform

Different platforms serve different purposes. Use them intentionally.

A blog post allows for long-form storytelling. Here you can explore more deeply by connecting photos with memories and combining logistics with understanding. This space allows you to explain the background behind your images, which suggest but don't fully reveal their stories.

Instagram is more visual and immediate. This platform allows you to display single images or produce a carousel that unfolds a visual story. A series can capture the development of a hike through its various stages or illustrate the changing colors of a sunset and the dynamic flow of a market day. Keep captions honest. Use the terms "hidden gem" or "off the beaten path" only if they stem from genuine personal discovery rather than following current trends.

Reels and stories provide an avenue to share moving moments. The energy of a festival and the serenity of snorkeling through coral reefs can be effectively captured with this technique as well as ferry rides across sunlit waters. Keep edits minimal. Allow the natural sounds of birdsong and laughter to carry the emotional weight of your content.

Community forums and Facebook create perfect platforms to exchange practical travel advice and connect with people who also seek immersive adventures. Use these platforms to suggest trustworthy local guides as well as sustainable tour options and accommodations that feel welcoming.

Whatever the platform, don't aim to impress. Aim to invite. Your reader or follower should feel like they're walking alongside you instead of receiving distant sales pitches.

Seeing with Intention

A camera has the power to preserve a moment but lacks the ability to convey its significance. That part is up to you.

The urge to photograph everything you witness while exploring Lanai and Molokai becomes almost irresistible. The landscapes will tempt you. The people will move you. The sky's colors will reach out to you. Your most significant photographs will emerge not from a pursuit of aesthetic appeal. They'll come from recognizing presence.

The images you capture during your stay hold value beyond mere saved memories. When you photograph your experiences, these images become visual offerings that recognize a welcoming place and its shared cultural rhythm as well as moments that encourage your awareness.

Let your storytelling be shaped by humility. Let your compositions be rooted in care. Frame your photographs to show the depth and integrity of your journey instead of collecting mere images.

The photographs you brought back from your journey will remind you of more than your travel destinations once you return home and clean the salt and dust off your skin and boots. The photographs become a vehicle to recall the depth of your presence during the journey.

That's the power of visual storytelling. The purpose of this photography is not to show you visited but to preserve who you transformed into during your time there.

Chapter Fifteen

Conclusion-The Story that Stays With You

When we first began this journey, I invited you to step away from the familiar and into a different rhythm—one marked not by urgency, but by presence. We explored Lanai and Molokai not through checklists, but through stories, quiet moments, and lived experiences that make these two islands something more than travel destinations. They are, in many ways, mirrors—offering reflections of a world that values stillness, stewardship, and sincerity.

Over the chapters of this guide, we hiked remote trails where the land seemed to speak, floated through crystal waters filled with vibrant life, and shared meals where every bite carried the memory of the soil it came from. We learned from farmers, artisans, musicians, and elders. We visited sacred sites and lingered under stars. And we were reminded, again and again, that Hawaii's magic doesn't lie only in its scenery but in its soul.

This book has been an exploration of Lanai and Molokai as they are meant to be experienced: slowly, intentionally, and respectfully. These islands are not playgrounds—they are living, breathing communities. Places where culture isn't curated for tourists but carried forward by people who practice it every day. That truth has guided every page you've read, and I hope it will shape every step you take from here.

What We've Discovered Together

From the very beginning, we looked at these islands not as exotic escapes, but as opportunities to reconnect—to land, to people, and to ourselves.

We discovered Lanai's rugged charm, where the Munro Trail winds through whispering forests and Shipwreck Beach tells stories in rusted metal and wind-blown sand. We saw how the island's transformation from plantation to luxury retreat has left behind both echoes and renewal—and how even with modern development, its stillness remains sacred.

Molokai invited us even deeper, into a space where Hawaiian culture beats strong and steady. We witnessed hula as prayer, taro farming as heritage, and storytelling as preservation. There were no large resorts, no fast-paced excursions—only truth, offered freely to those willing to slow down and listen.

We traveled through outdoor adventures and cultural ceremonies, sampled local dishes passed down through generations, and wandered off the beaten path toward hidden waterfalls, secluded beaches, and hillside farms where aloha means more than "hello"—it means "you are welcome here."

What It All Means

Throughout this book, certain themes rose again and again. They weren't manufactured—they revealed themselves in the lived experience of these islands. Now, as we close, I want to bring those themes forward one more time.

Cultural immersion is the gateway to understanding: We've seen how deeply Hawaiian values shape the way people live on Lanai and Molokai. From the sacred act of lei-making to the communal spirit of taro harvesting, culture is not decoration here—it is foundation. And when travelers approach that culture with humility and curiosity, it opens doors that no tour can unlock.

Sustainability isn't a travel trend—it's a necessity: In places as delicate as these islands, every footprint counts. We talked about reef-safe sunscreen, local farming, Leave No Trace principles, and the importance of participating in conservation work. But even more than tips, we explored a mindset: that we are not separate from nature, but part of it—and therefore responsible for how we move through it.

Adventure isn't always loud: Yes, there are hikes and kayaks and snorkeling expeditions. But there's also the quiet thrill of a local storyteller's voice, the stillness of a forest after rain, the soft hush of waves at dawn. Lanai and Molokai teach us that adventure doesn't always mean adrenaline. Sometimes, it means paying attention.

Lessons to Carry Into Future Travels

I expect you to utilize the insights you've acquired here in future journeys beyond this particular trip. Let them travel with you.

One should take the Aloha Spirit beyond the airport terminal. This approach to interaction through compassion and generosity combined with an open heart changes our global experience wherever we travel.

Traditional Hawaiian knowledge—from sustainable land management to intergenerational storytelling—demonstrates that wisdom remains deeply connected to local traditions and elders. During our travels to both distant and local communities we should carry the same level of respect and openness to truly listen.

Our genuine interactions with local people revealed that authenticity depends on emotional resonance rather than visual appearance. Authenticity emerges during spontaneous dialogues while eating together and when people experience mutual understanding. Travel becomes meaningful when it becomes relational.

An Invitation to Travel Differently

If there's one call to action I want to leave you with, it's this: Let your future travels reflect what you've learned here..

Support community-led programs alongside family-owned businesses and cultural education initiatives during your travels. Be a guest, not a consumer. Ask questions. Give back when you can. Never take items like shells or photos from sacred sites or tell stories that aren't yours.

Sustainable travel requires awareness rather than striving for perfection. It's about awareness. Your travels should ideally result in positive change, but at minimum they should not disturb the places you visit.

Traveling with respect makes the world appear far more giving. It opens up. It reveals things you could never find in any planned itinerary.

Let's Keep the Conversation Going

When this guide triggers any form of thought or recollection in you or leads to unexpected reflections, please take the time to share those experiences. Tell your story. Share the identities of people you encountered and the locations which inspired you, along with lessons you continue to discover.

There's a quiet community of travelers out there—those who seek meaning, not just mileage. And every story shared adds to that community's wisdom.

Whether it's through writing, conversation, or another visit, keep the dialogue alive. The more we share, the more we protect what's real.

One Last Story

When I first arrived on Molokai, I wandered into a local craft fair tucked behind a small church. There was no sign out front—just music, laughter, and the smell of something sweet in the air. I bought a handmade bracelet from a woman who told me it took her three days to weave. "You wear it," she said, "when you need to remember where you belong."

At the time, I didn't fully understand what she meant. But over time, I've come to realize she wasn't talking about geography. She was talking about presence. About connection. About being rooted, even as you move.

I still wear that bracelet when I travel. And every time I do, I remember the lesson these islands teach so well: that the richest parts of the journey aren't about where you go—they're about how deeply you choose to be there.

Thank you for choosing to be here. I hope this isn't the end of your journey—only a beautiful pause before the next beginning.

Ready to keep exploring?

If you enjoyed this guide, you can also listen to the audiobook version on Audible. It's perfect for travel days, road trips, or brushing up on your plans while on the go.

You can also explore more destinations through our full library of narrated guides at:
www.audible.com/oceanbreezeadventures

Wherever you go next, we'll be with you every step of the way.

Continue Your Island Adventure

Love this guide? Explore the complete **Ocean Breeze Adventures Hawaii Series**, created to help you plan stress-free trips to every major island.

Oʻahu Travel & Adventure Guide - The Gathering Place: nightlife, culture, and iconic beaches.

Maui Travel & Adventure Guide - The Valley Isle: adventure, romance, and breathtaking drives.

Kauaʻi Travel & Adventure Guide - The Garden Isle: waterfalls, tranquility, and endless greenery.

Big Island Travel & Adventure Guide - The Orchid Isle: volcanoes, diversity, and discovery.

Lānaʻi and Molokai Travel & Adventure Guide - The Pineapple & Friendly Isles: quiet escapes, local culture, and authentic aloha.

Discover your perfect island match or learn more about each destination at **www.OceanBreezeAdventures.com**

Stay Connected

Join the Ocean Breeze community to receive travel updates, planning tips, and destination inspiration for your next adventure.
Sign up at **www.OceanBreezeAdventures.com**

About Ocean Breeze Adventures

At **Ocean Breeze Adventures**, travel isn't just about getting away—it's about creating stories that stay with you.
Founded by author and travel designer **Diana Freel**, Ocean Breeze Adventures blends expert knowledge, insider insight, and a genuine passion for discovery to help travelers explore the world with confidence, curiosity, and heart.

For more travel inspiration and destination guides, visit
www.OceanBreezeAdventures.com

Ocean Breeze Adventures Travel Agency

At **Ocean Breeze Adventures**, travel isn't just about getting away—it's about creating stories that stay with you.
Our mission is to make exploring the world effortless, authentic, and deeply memorable.

Founded by author and travel designer **Diana Freel**, Ocean Breeze Adventures blends expert knowledge, insider insight, and a genuine passion for discovery to help travelers experience destinations in meaningful ways.

From the beaches of Hawaii to the rainforests of Costa Rica and the glaciers of Alaska, Ocean Breeze Adventures inspires travelers to explore with confidence, curiosity, and heart.

For more travel inspiration and destination guides, visit
www.OceanBreezeAdventures.com

www.ingramcontent.com/pod-product-compliance
Lightning Source LLC
Chambersburg PA
CBHW062108080426
42734CB00012B/2799